Library of
Davidson College

VOID

PROFILE OF THE LAST PURITAN

American Academy of Religion
Academy Series

edited by
Susan Thistlethwaite

I. Self-love p. 39, 40 (see Self-Reliance)
II Beauty p. 64 (see Nature)

Number 73
PROFILE OF THE LAST PURITAN

by
David C. Brand

David C. Brand

PROFILE OF THE LAST PURITAN
Jonathan Edwards, Self-Love, and the Dawn of the Beatific

Scholars Press
Atlanta, Georgia

PROFILE OF THE LAST PURITAN

by
David C. Brand

© 1991
The American Academy of Religion

Scripture quotations in the main body of the text are taken from the HOLY BIBLE, NEW INTERNATIONAL VERSION © 1973, 1978 by the International Bible Society, used by permission of Zondervan Bible Publishers.

Library of Congress Cataloging in Publication Data

Brand, David C.
    Profile of the last Puritan : Jonathan Edwards, self-love, and the dawn of the beatific / David C. Brand.
    p. cm. — (American Academy of religion academy series ; no. 73)
    Includes bibliographical references and index.
    ISBN 1-55540-582-7 (hard : alk paper). — ISBN 1-55540-583-5 (pbk. : alk paper)
    1. Edwards, Jonathan, 1703-1758. 2. Puritans—United States. 3. Self-acceptance—Religious aspects—Christianity. 4. Beatific vision. 5. Arminianism—History. 6. Philosophical theology—History of doctrines—18th century. I. Title. II. Series.
BX7260.E3872   1991
285.8'092—dc20   91-7420
                                                                                       CIP

Printed in the United States of America
on acid-free paper

To James L. Gaupp,
beloved father-in-law,
twentieth-century patriarch
of the faith, and long-time
faithful friend

TABLE OF CONTENTS

PREFACE ix

INTRODUCTION 1

    Statement of Thesis 1

    Development of Thesis 2

    Definition of Terms 3

CHAPTER

I.   EDWARDS THE MAN 5

    The Puritan Setting 5

    The Personal Biography 9

    The Philosophical Perspective 24

II.   MORAL PHILOSOPHY AND THE BENEVOLIST SCHOOL 31

    Pietistic Backgrounds of Benevolism 31

    The Cartesian Revolution 37

    The Benevolist School 45

III.	BENEVOLENCE AND THE BEATIFIC	55
	Objectivism in Edwards	55
	Ethics and Aesthetics	59
	Disinterested Benevolence versus Self-Love	65
	Holiness and Happiness	73
IV.	CALVIN, THE COVENANT, AND THE BEATIFIC	79
	Edwards and Dort's Five Points	79
	Neoplatonistic Tendencies	84
	Covenantal Structure	89
V.	BENEVOLENCE AND ARMINIANISM	111
	Rationalist Arminian Benevolism	111
	"Consistent Calvinism"	124
	Benevolist Arminian Evangelicalism	130
CONCLUSION		145
	Synopsis	145
	The Legacy of Edwards	146
APPENDIX		149
	Edwards and the "Lapsarian" Issue	149
REFERENCE LIST		153
INDEX		159

Preface

One Sunday afternoon, more than a few years ago, I was voicing disapproval of (what I regarded as) my boyhood friend's idolatrous religious practices: "The first commandment says, 'Thou shalt have no other gods before me.'" I can still remember my friend's response: "It sounds like God is trying to 'hog' the whole show." In many ways the chapters that follow represent a theological resolution of my friend's comment. To put it in Edwardsean terms, this book has emerged from the author's crisis of *"personal identity"* whereby the experiences of youth and adulthood are divinely established as an unbroken chain of consciousness (Edwards 1879, 1:224-25).

"For in him we live and move and have our being" (Acts 17:28 NIV).

Profile of the Last Puritan is a reflection of the author's spiritual roots; indeed, it represents an intensive look at the religious roots of America. The profound theological themes of Jonathan Edwards draw attention, by way of contrast, to a certain spiritual and theological impoverishment currently afflicting the American church.

The reader will discover in Edwards the theological grist to confront the fashionable gods of the human "self," to correct the modern existentialist concept of "being," and to alter the face of modern historical criticism.

Rudolph Bultmann postulated a concept of history as a "closed continuum" which "cannot be rent by the interference of supernatural, transcendent powers," but which, nevertheless, allows for "free" human decisions:

> But even a free decision does not happen without cause, without a motive; and the task of the historian is to come to know the motives of actions (Ladd 1967, 183).

Edwards's concept of "motive" as determinate cause of action (1879, 1:5-8, 12, 30) applies directly to Bultmann's description of the historian's task, and is sufficient to reconstruct Bultmann's concept of history on a theistic base.

Dr. Daniel P. Fuller first introduced me to the theological writing of Edwards in a senior class seminar on "The Unity of the Bible" at Fuller Theological Seminary in 1967. On the list of required reading was Edwards's *Dissertation Concerning the End for Which God Created the World*, a work which I have come to regard as unsurpassed in terms of its theological grandeur.

The chapters that follow were written as a Th.M. thesis completed at Westminster Theological Seminary in Philadelphia in the spring of 1988. I am especially grateful to Dr. Samuel T. Logan, Jr., Academic Dean of Westminster Theological Seminary, who as my advisor encouraged this endeavor and nominated my thesis for publication. Dr. Logan and his colleagues introduced me to the riches of the Reformed and Puritan heritage.

My research has been richly rewarded through the contributions of many different authors, and I am indebted to their scholarly labors. Perry Miller's monumental contribution to the modern interest in Puritan studies, and to the study of Jonathan Edwards in particular, must not go unmentioned. The most valuable study in unlocking the Puritan sage's thought, other than Edwards's own writings, has been Norman Fiering's two-volume work, indeed a landmark of scholarship devoid of the bias that so frequently taints works on Edwards.

Preface

I extend my appreciation to the congregation of Emmanuel Baptist Church in Atlantic Highlands, New Jersey, who afforded me the privilege of academic study while serving as a pastor.

The professional typing and word-processing expertise offered as a labor of love by Wally and Nancy Memmer during the thesis stage have been invaluable. J. Michael Brandon's literary talents were especially helpful in critiquing the conclusion and other portions of my thesis. Ron McRae and Sandra Johnson have assisted this project to publication readiness with their constructive comments and word-processing skills. Tom Darnell has helped oversee the final stages of word processing. Dr. John Gerstner's scholarly criticism in the pre-publication stage has been greatly appreciated.

I am grateful to Dr. Susan Thistlethwaite and her colleagues of the American Academy of Religion for their acceptance of this work for publication. Dr. Robert Hauck, Assistant Editor of Scholars Press Academy Series, has offered gracious assistance and counsel in manuscript preparation.

I express my affectionate appreciation to my wife Marilyn whose "calmness and universal benevolence of mind" have endured the rigors of this project and who has been my most devoted human companion during the last twenty-six years; to Mark whose challenging mind helped motivate me to graduate study and who has been an excellent "sounding board"; to Sara, whose sweet, benevolent spirit has been a constant joy and refreshment to our entire family; to Jonathan who encouraged me to "go for it"; and to Scott who has preserved me from getting too "heavenly-minded" while on this planet.

Praise be to the God of all grace and glory who has redeemed me from his eternal wrath, the just desert of my sin, who continues to have mercy, and who will sustain me until that glorious Day!

Introduction

Statement of Thesis

In many respects Jonathan Edwards was the last true Puritan. Certainly his writings represent the high-water mark of New England theology, both in terms of a systematic summons to the original Puritan dream envisioned by Massachusetts Bay founder John Winthrop, and of a touchstone of theological excellence and expression unequalled by subsequent generations of pastors and theologians.

Edwards's life and writings reflect the dawn of the beatific--"the imperfect beginnings of a blessed and endless sight of God" (Edwards 1879, 2:910), and indeed can scarcely be construed on any other basis.

> The saints in this world have an earnest of what is future, they have the dawnings of future light . . .
> The discoveries which the saints here have of God's excellency and grace, are immediate in a sense; that is, they do not mainly consist of ratiocination; but yet in another sense they are indirect, that is, they are by means of the gospel, as through a glass; but in heaven God will immediately excite apprehensions of himself, without the use of any such means (Edwards 1879, 2:907).

Motivated by a spiritual foretaste of beatific vision rooted objectively in Holy Scripture, Edwards projected the major unifying theme of his life and works--the glory of God--against the backdrop raised by the man-centered moral philosophers of his day, and against a rising Arminian tide. Indeed he employed the language and idiom of the moral philosophers for his own spiritual-theological purpose.

Though Perry Miller well conceded Jonathan Edwards to be "the greatest philosopher-theologian yet to grace the American scene," Edwards's demonstrated greatness as a philosopher was incidental to his task as a pastor-theologian (Bogue 1975, 3). Norman Fiering accurately depicted Edwards's engagements with secular philosophy as debates on the steps of the temple, merely interesting preliminaries to the sacred truths inside, which "he held to undeviatingly" (Fiering 1981a, 49). Though Edwards's peers and subsequent theologians made concessions to the demands of an anthropocentric empirical psychology that regarded ethics as an autonomous discipline, Edwards held up theology as the "queen of the sciences" (Bogue 1975, chap. 3).

Edwards viewed benevolence and self-love, properly defined, as mutually compatible. In reference to man, the latter was properly subordinate to the former; in reference to God, the former to the latter--indeed God's benevolence consisted primarily in his self-love.

Development of Thesis

Chapter 1 explores Edwards's Puritan roots, describes his conversion and its relationship to his life and thought, and defines his role as a philosopher.

Chapter 2 documents the moral-philosophical landscape against which Edwards set his theological message.

Chapter 3 which, along with Chapter 4, represents the heart of the book, relates the beatific and the benevolent by highlighting a series of critical issues: ethics and aesthetics, disinterested benevolence and self-love, and happiness and holiness.

Chapter 4 establishes the Calvinistic and covenantal underpinnings of Edwards's theology which relate thematically to the beatific and issue supremely in the glory of God.

Chapter 5 traces the development of Arminianism in New England as an accelerated reaction to Edwards and the Great Awakening, and as proceeding hand-in-hand with a man-centered doctrine of benevolence. Its triumph is shown to be complete in the rise of Unitarianism on the one hand, and in a broadening evangelicalism on the other, the latter epitomized by the theology of Edwards's grandson Timothy Dwight, Yale president and leader in the Second Great Awakening.

Definition of Terms

"Beatific" (Edwards 1879, 2:906), strictly defined, refers to that perfect, blessed, and immediate sight of God reserved for the saints in heavenly glory (1 Cor 13:12; 1 Jn 3:2), of which the transforming experience of regeneration and sanctification in this present life is the spiritual dawning (2 Cor 3:18; 1 Jn 1:14; Acts 7:55-56).

> The more perfect view which the saints have of God's glory and love in another world, is what is especially called the seeing of God. Then they shall see him as he is. The light which is now but a glimmering, will be brought to clear sunshine; that which is here but the dawning, will become perfect day (Edwards 1879, 2:907).

In keeping with the above definition, "beatific" in the following chapters will have frequent application to the spiritual life of the Christian believer in this present age, insomuch as such a life is an expression, albeit an imperfect one, of the heavenly from which it radiates.

"Benevolence" will be taken variously as a disposition, or action, toward the happiness, welfare, or good of another (or others) in contrast to malevolence, a disposition or action toward the misery of another (or others). "Benevolist" will describe that school of eighteenth-century sentimentalist moral philosophy which regarded the human will via benevolent feelings as naturally inclined toward benevolence. "Sentimentalism," which Norman Fiering cited as "the most significant development in the history of ethics between 1675 and 1725," represented that branch of moral philosophy that emphasized the constructive role of the feelings (affections and passions); "intellectualism" had made the cognitive faculties of reason, intellect, and understanding the determinate factors in moral behavior (1981b, 5; 1981a, 10). The "Cartesian Revolution" refers to that period of history precipitated by the famous dictum of Rene Descartes (1596-1650), *Cogito, ergo sum* ("I think; therefore, I am") which ushered in the modern age of moral philosophy based on empirical observation of sensory experience coupled with inductive reasoning (Latourette 1953, 692).

The term Arminian designates that body of Christian theology which stands opposed to the system known as Calvinism. Though there are, to be sure, various degrees and shades of Arminianism, Arminianism generally accentuated human freedom rather than divine sovereignty. More particularly, Arminianism denied the doctrines affirmed at the Synod of Dort, viz., total depravity, unconditional election, limited atonement, irresistible grace, and the perseverance of the saints--which doctrines shall, in the following chapters, represent that system known as "Calvinism" (Steele and Thomas 1963; Heimert and Miller 1967, xiii-xiv).

Covenant (or covenantal) theology designates the more fully developed system of Calvinistic thought embodied in the Westminster Standards which regarded the covenant as the hermeneutic key or the dominant organizing principle of theology (Letham 1986). The expression "New Divinity" derogatorily described the followers of Jonathan Edwards, such as Samuel Hopkins, Samuel Buell, Joseph Bellamy, and Jonathan Edwards, Jr., who regarded themselves as "consistent Calvinists" and who attempted to assert Edwardsean principles of theology over against the Arminian tide during the latter half of the eighteenth century after Edwards's death (Conforti, 1981, 3, 30, 38).

Although the history of philosophy and theology in Puritan New England, and Jonathan Edwards's relationship to it, are complex (necessitating further definition of terms), the major issues are relatively simple--indeed reducible to benevolence, self-love, and the dawn of the beatific.

CHAPTER I

EDWARDS THE MAN

The Puritan Setting

The life of Jonathan Edwards cannot be adequately understood or appreciated without an introduction to Puritan New England whose origins can be traced to the story of John Winthrop and the establishment of the holy commonwealth--and before that to Puritanism in old England. Alan Simpson in his book *Puritanism in Old and New England* defined, somewhat sardonically, what he regarded as the distinguishing feature of Puritanism:

> The essence of Puritanism--what Cromwell called "the root of the matter" when he surveyed the whole unruly flock--is an experience of conversion which separates the Puritan from the mass of mankind and endows him with the privileges and the duties of the elect. The root of the matter is always a new birth, which brings with it a conviction of salvation and a dedication to warfare against sin. . . .
> The whole object of the Puritan's existence was to trace its course in himself and to produce it in others ([1955] 1966, 2).

Citing C. H. Firth's *Oliver Cromwell*, Simpson indicated (as a footnote) that qualifications for ministerial status in Cromwell's state church were based on "the root of the matter" rather than a man's ecclesiastical status--whether Presbyterian, Independent, or Baptist.

Although Puritans on both sides of the Atlantic were agreed that man's chief end was "to glorify God, and to enjoy him for ever" (Committee n.d., Sh. Cat., Q. 1; Walker [1893] 1960, 194-95), there can be no doubt that the "root" of their tensions with English royalty was the matter of the conversion experience. Some had hoped for an English duplication of Calvin's Geneva, heralded by John Knox as "the most perfect school of Christ that ever was in the earth since the days of the apostles" (Knappen [1939], 1966, 136). The church in Geneva had had a presbyterian form of government as opposed to the English prelacy, a government-appointed episcopal hierarchy (Knappen [1939], 1966, 134-48; Haller [1938] 1984, 173). Others, who came to be known as Congregationalists, insisted that Calvin had not gone far enough concerning the matter of church discipline, and they pressed for a church membership which required a profession of "historical" faith (statement of doctrinal orthodoxy), a morally upright life, and assent to a covenant (Morgan [1963], 1982, 20-63).

Among those who held to the congregational principle of government were the Separatists (those who desired to break away from the Church of England) some of whom sailed to Plymouth, Massachusetts under the leadership of William Bradford and Elder William Brewster after having fled to Leyden, Holland where they sat under the ministry of John Robinson. Others, however, were Non-Separating Congregationalists who refused to break their ties with the Church of England. It was from this latter group that the Massachusetts Bay Colony was formed under the godly leadership of John Winthrop who, with a charter from Charles I in hand, set forth aboard the *Arbella*, on March 29, 1630, to found a holy commonwealth in New England (Ahlstrom 1972, 135-39, 144-45; Morgan 1958, 45-83).

The harmonious relationship which the Separatist Pilgrims of Plymouth were to enjoy with their Non-Separatist Puritan brethren at Massachusetts Bay can be traced to the moderating influence that William Ames (1576-1633), exiled Cambridge scholar, Puritan preacher, and protege of William Perkins, had had upon John Robinson in Holland (Ames [1629] 1983, 1-10).

The Puritans of Massachusetts Bay bound themselves together in obedience to God in terms of a national covenant.

> There is . . . a double law by which we are regulated . . . the law of nature and the law of grace, or the moral law or [and?] the law of the Gospel. . . .
> The law of nature was given to man in the estate of innocency, this of the Gospel in the estate of regeneracy. . . .
> We ought to account ourselves knit together by this bond of love. . . .
> The end is to improve our lives to do more service to the Lord, the comfort and increase of the body of Christ whereof we are members, that ourselves and our posterity may be the better preserved from the common corruptions of this evil world. . . .
> That which the most in churches maintain as a truth in profession only, we must bring into familiar and constant practice: as in this duty of love. . . .
> Thus stands the cause between God and us: we are entered into covenant with Him for this work. . . . Now if the Lord shall be pleased to hear us and bring us in peace to the place we desire, then hath He ratified this covenant and sealed our commission, [and] will expect a strict performance of the articles contained in it. . . .
> We shall find that the God of Israel is among us, when ten of us shall be able to resist a thousand of our enemies, when He shall make us a praise and glory, that men shall say of succeeding plantations: "The Lord make it like that of New England." For we must consider that we shall be as a city on a hill, the eyes of all people are upon us (Miller [1956], 1982, 80-83).

When the Massachusetts Bay Colony was established, the voting franchise was confined to church members. By 1635, through the influence of John Cotton, pastor of the Boston congregation, a personal "narrative of grace" (attesting to one's salvation experience) was made a requirement for church membership in Massachusetts Bay. In March of 1636 the Massachusetts Bay General Court enacted a law forbidding the formation of any church without the prior consent of the civil magistrates and the elders of the majority of the churches within the jurisdiction of Massachusetts Bay (Morgan [1963] 1982, 99-105). Thus, in Massachusetts Bay, unlike any other place on the earth, was a society governed by "visible saints"--those who were bound by a church covenant, whose lives were morally upright (in the charitable judgment of the church), who were doctrinally orthodox, and, most uniquely, who could give satisfactory testimony of a *personal salvation experience.*

This concept of a holy commonwealth based on visible sainthood was to undergo a severe test during the Antinomian controversy when Anne Hutchinson charged that all but two of the New England clergy were under a "covenant of works." She insisted that sanctification (a visibly upright life) was not a necessary evidence of justification. She would be banished from the colony on the ground of treason and later ex-communicated from the Boston church (Winthrop 1908, 1:195-273; Higgins 1984).

New England Puritans were to insist on the "congregational way" as distinct from the presbyterian system of their Westminster brethren in England. While they endorsed the Westminster confessional standards, they set forth their own Cambridge Platform in 1648 which spelled out their unique system of congregational government (Walker [1893] 1960, 194-237).

Puritanism in New England underwent a radical change in 1662 when the Half-Way Covenant was introduced which allowed parents to have their children baptized, even though those second and third generation parents were unable to give a "narrative of grace," as long as their lives were free from scandal and their doctrine was orthodox (Miller [1953] 1983, 95-104).

A letter from King Charles II on June 28, 1662 demanded provision for use of the Book of Common Prayer, insisted that persons of honest lives be admitted to the Lord's Supper, and extended the voting franchise to all landowners whose religion was orthodox. On October 23, 1684 Charles II annulled the Massachusetts Bay Charter. The New England Puritan national covenant scheme was broken.

Cotton Mather's attempt to create a consociation of churches in the Boston area, in order to salvage what remained of the corporate Puritan vision, failed because of an unwillingness on the part of individual pastors and churches to surrender their new independence which had come with "Toleration." The consociation movement was more successful in the Connecticut Valley, however, due in large part to the powerful influence of the "Pope" of Connecticut Valley, Solomon Stoddard. The adoption of the Saybrook Platform in 1708, the fruit of Stoddard's labors, provided a semi-presbyterian basis for Puritanism to conserve its spiritual heritage in a corporate way, and was later to bring New England Puritans into greater ecclesiastical proximity with the Presbyterians in the Middle Colonies (Miller [1953] 1983, 126-29, 146, 265-67; [1949] 1973, 9-12).

Stoddard's ministry as the pastor of the Northampton church from 1669 to his death in 1729 was attended with the blessing of several spiritual "harvests." Stoddard, in his desire to preach to the unconverted, and believing the Lord's Supper to be a converting ordinance, persuaded his congregation to expand the boundaries of the Half-Way Covenant even further by admitting to the Lord's Supper those who were unable to give a personal "narrative of grace," as long as they were not guilty of any heresy or scandal. Other churches rapidly followed (Miller [1953] 1983, 226-67, 235-36). It was into this Puritan New England that Jonathan Edwards was born, and it was Solomon Stoddard's pulpit that he was to occupy for twenty-three years. It was the central Puritan issue of conversion, and the validation of that experience, that was to occupy so much of his ministry and become the subject of his writings. And finally, it was the relationship between the "narrative of grace" and church membership that was to become the issue of his dismissal from the pastorate at Northampton.

The Personal Biography

Jonathan Edwards was born in the East Windsor parsonage October 5, 1703 to Timothy and Esther Edwards. His father had matriculated at Harvard College receiving his degree in 1694. Timothy Edwards began his pastoral ministry in East Windsor that same year and would continue preaching there until his death just prior to his son's. Jonathan's mother, Esther, was the daughter of Solomon Stoddard, influential and esteemed pastor of the Northampton parish. She would live in the East Windsor parsonage until her death at the age of ninety-eight. John Wesley was born in England during the same year as Edwards's birth, though they would never personally meet (Winslow [1940] 1979, 20-28).

Four sisters were born prior to Jonathan, and six sisters followed, but he would be the only son. Jonathan's childhood was characterized by an intense interest in nature, a rigorous program of instruction in Bible, Greek and Latin, along with other boys, under the instruction of his father, and the witnessing of, and delight in, at least two seasons of revival at East Windsor (Murray 1987, 10-19). Concerning the times of revival, Edwards was to reflect many years later:

> I had a variety of concerns and exercises about my soul from childhood; but I had two more remarkable seasons of awakening, before I met with that change by which I was brought to those new dispositions, and that new sense of things, that I have since had. The first time was when I was a boy, some years before I went to college, at a time of remarkable awakening in my father's congregation. I was then very much affected for many months, and concerned about the things of religion, and my soul's salvation; and was abundant in religious duties. I used to pray five times a day in secret, and to spend much time in religious conversation with other boys; and used to meet with them to pray together. I experienced I know not what kind of delight in religion. My mind was much engaged in it, and had much self-righteous pleasure, and it was my delight to abound in religious duties. I, with some of my school-mates, joined together and built a booth in a swamp, in a very retired spot, for a place of prayer. And besides, I had particular secret places of my own in the woods, where I used to retire by myself; and was from time to time much affected. My affections seemed to be lively and easily moved, and I seemed to be in my element when I engaged in religious duties. And I am ready to think, many are deceived with such affections, and such a kind of delight as I then had in religion, and mistake it for grace (1879, vol. 1, p. liv).

Edwards, in contrasting this childhood, temporary "season of awakening" with his conversion some time later, described his authentic conversion as characterized by "new dispositions" and a "new sense of things" in contrast to a kind of preoccupation with "religious duties" and "self-righteous pleasures" devoid of "grace." This was significant for three reasons, each of which is germane to the thesis of this book. First of all, the use of the expressions "new dispositions" and "new sense of things" are terms which bespoke Edwards's acquaintance with the language of the seventeenth- and eighteenth-century world of moral philosophy, as well as his willingness to employ that language in describing the biblical experience of regeneration. Secondly, his clear distinction between the true experience of "grace" and "self-righteous pleasure" revealed his Calvinistic understanding of the Christian faith.

Chapter 1 11

Thirdly, though his affections were "lively" and very prominent in this religious awakening experience, there did not appear to have been any benevolent quality in those affections but only self-love as the expression "self-righteous pleasure" suggests.

Iain Murray cited another remarkable outpouring of the Spirit of God upon the East Windsor congregation mentioned by Edwards in a letter written to his sister Mary while she was visiting relatives at Hadley. At that time about thirteen members were added to the congregation (1987, 20).

Edwards entered the Collegiate School at Connecticut (later named "Yale") in September, 1716, and studied under the tutelage of Elisha Williams at Wethersfield until a leadership crisis at New Haven was resolved with the replacement of Samuel Johnson by Timothy Cutler. Johnson had apparently become so enamored with the "new philosophy" of Descartes, Boyle, Locke, and Newton that his theology had deteriorated.

While at Yale (so named after its chief benefactor in 1718) Edwards, along with other students, recited the Westminster Shorter Catechism every Saturday evening and participated in daily and weekly times of worship, prayer, and reading of Scripture which went hand-in-hand with the more academic curriculum of geometry, astronomy, the art of thinking, and mathematics. As the top ranking student in his class, he gave the Farewell Oration at Commencement in September of 1720. Thereafter he continued at Yale so as to complete his Master of Arts in divinity in 1722 at which time he received a call to pastor a Presbyterian church in New York City (Murray 1987, 25-41).

In his *Memoirs* Edwards described what constituted for him the beginning of the effectual operation of God's saving grace in his own life in contrast to the temporary childhood season of awakening described above. According to his personal account, the authentic conversion experience took place approximately a year and a half before he went to New York. He recounted how the doctrine of God's sovereign election had raised many questions in his mind since childhood--indeed it had appeared to be "a horrible doctrine" to him (Edwards 1879, vol. 1, pp. liv-lvi; Murray 1987, 35).

> But I remember the time very well when I seemed to be convinced, and fully satisfied, as to this sovereignty of God, and his justice in thus eternally disposing of men, according to his sovereign pleasure. But never could I give an account how, or by what means, I was thus convinced, nor in the least imagining at the time, nor a long time after, that there was any extraordinary influence of God's Spirit in it; but only that now I saw further, and my reason apprehended the justice and reasonableness of it. However, my mind rested in it; and it put an end to all those cavils and objections. And there has been a wonderful alteration in my mind, with respect to the doctrine of God's sovereignty, from that day to this; so that I scarce ever have found so much as the rising of an objection against it, in the most absolute sense, in God's showing mercy to whom he will show mercy, and hardening whom he will (1879, vol. 1, pp. liv-lv).

Edwards went on to speak of the new inward joy that had replaced the terror he once had experienced concerning God's sovereignty. In so speaking he must surely have been expressing the "new sense of things," as he had put it, in contrasting "grace" with "self-righteous pleasure."

> I have often, since that first conviction, had quite another kind of sense of God's sovereignty than I had then. I have often since had not only a conviction, but a *delightful* conviction. The doctrine has very often appeared exceedingly pleasant, bright, and sweet. Absolute sovereignty is what I love to ascribe to God (1879, vol. 1, p. lv).

Again Edwards's description was noteworthy because (1) he described the experience of regeneration in the language of the "senses," and (2) the Calvinistic doctrine of "absolute sovereignty" was the truth that especially delighted him. The objective nature of Edwards's regenerative experience was evident from his account of the moment in which he was first conscious of this majestic sweetness within his soul.

> The first instance, that I remember, of that sort of inward, sweet delight in God and divine things, that I have lived much in since, was on reading those words, 1 Tim i:17. *Now unto the King eternal, immortal, invisible, the only wise God, be honour and glory for ever and ever. Amen.* As I read the words, there came into my soul, and was as it were diffused through it, a sense of the glory of the Divine Being; a new sense, quite different from any thing I ever experienced

before. Never any words of Scripture seemed to me as these
words did. I thought with myself, how excellent a Being that
was, and how happy I should be, if I might enjoy that God,
and be rapt up to Him in heaven; and be as it were swallowed
up in him forever! I kept saying, and as it were singing, over
these words of Scripture to myself; and went to pray to God
that I might enjoy him; and prayed in a manner quite different
from what I used to do, with a new sort of affection. But it
never came into my thought, that there was any thing
spiritual, or of a saving nature in this (1879, vol. 1, p. lv).

The above passage described the affectional progression from an inner satisfaction and peace regarding the truth of the doctrine of God's sovereign election (a central Calvinistic doctrine) to the rapturous enjoyment of, and basking of the soul in, the Divine Presence through contemplation of the words of Scripture. This was not a mere subjective, mystical experience, but an objective experience rooted in the Bible. As Edwards went on to describe the spiritual reality which he encountered in regeneration he came close to uttering "inexpressible things, things that man is not permitted to tell" (2 Cor 12:4 NIV).

From about that time I began to have a new kind of
apprehensions and ideas of Christ, and the work of
redemption, and the glorious way of salvation by him. An
inward sweet sense of these things, at times, came into my
heart; and my soul was led away in pleasant views and
contemplations of them. And my mind was greatly engaged
to spend my time in reading and meditating on Christ, on the
beauty and excellency of his person, and the lovely way of
salvation by free grace in him. I found no books so delightful
to me as those that treated of these subjects. Those words
Cant. ii. 1. used to be abundantly with me. *I am the rose of
Sharon, and the lily of the valleys.* The words seemed to me
sweetly to represent the loveliness and beauty of Jesus Christ.
The whole book of Canticles used to be pleasant to me, and
I used to be much in reading it, about that time; and found
from time to time an inward sweetness, that would carry me
away in my contemplations (1879, vol. 1, p. lv).

In contemplating these words, descriptive of things beyond the physical senses, and yet in the language of the senses, one might think that Edwards had been influenced by John Cotton's writings.

> Let me . . . teach Christians not to be afraid of the word *Revelation*: you have heard of many that have attended to *Revelation*, that have been deceived: it is true for the Devil will transform himself into an angel of light: he will be foisting in many delusions, yea, many times when the soul waiteth for the revelation of God's mercy, the Devil will be apt to foist in such revelations, from which many delusions grow: but yet on the other side, let not men be afraid, and say, that we have no *revelation* but the *word*: for I do believe and do confidently affirm, that if there were no revelation but the word, there would be no spiritual grace revealed to the soul: for it is more than the letter of the word that is required to it: not that I look for any other matter besides the word. . . . True it is indeed, whether the *Father*, *Son*, or *Spirit* reveal any thing, it is in and according to the *word*: but without the work of the *Spirit* there is no faith begotten by any promise (Cotton 1671, 177-78).

Probably Cotton had in mind Paul's prayer in the Letter to the Ephesians in telling Christians not to fear the word revelation (Eph 1:17). Certainly both Cotton's counsel and Edwards's described beatific sensations were clearly within the bounds of historic Calvinistic theology.

Calvin had affirmed the indissoluble relationship between the Word and the Spirit and, at the same time, the indispensability of each. In reference to the Holy Spirit Calvin said,

> But lest under his sign the spirit of Satan should creep in, he would have us recognize him in his own image, which he has stamped upon the Scriptures. He is the Author of the Scriptures: he cannot vary and differ from himself (1960, 1:94-95).

> For by a kind of mutual bond the Lord has joined together the certainty of his Word and of his Spirit so that the perfect religion of the Word may abide in our minds when the Spirit, who causes us to contemplate God's face, shines; and that we in turn may embrace the Spirit with no fear of being deceived when we recognize him in his own image, namely in the Word. So indeed it is. God did not bring the Word among men for the sake of a momentary display, intending at the coming of the Spirit to abolish it. Rather, he sent down the same Spirit by whose power he dispensed the Word, to complete his work by the efficacious confirmation of the Word (1960, 1:95).

Edwards's rapturous contemplations were an exercise in aesthetics as he spoke of the "beauty and excellency" of Christ's person and the "lovely way of salvation by free grace in him." Nevertheless, their arising from a study of the Song of Solomon would seem to be precisely that kind of experience which Calvin ascribed to the ministry of the Holy Spirit in the above passages. Edwards's experience of the beatific, however ineffable, had Christ as its focus and Holy Scripture as its foundation.

> This I know not how to express otherwise, than by a calm, sweet abstraction of soul from all the concerns of this world; and sometimes a kind of vision, or fixed ideas and imaginations, of being along in the mountains, or some sweet solitary wilderness, far from all mankind, sweetly conversing with Christ, and wrapt and swallowed up in God. The sense I had of divine things, would often of a sudden kindle up, as it were, a sweet burning in my heart, an ardour of soul, that I know not how to express (Edwards 1879, vol. 1, p. lv).

Iain Murray located the time of Edwards's conversion sometime shortly after March 1, 1721, noting the absence of any reference to the experience in a letter Edwards had written to his father on that date. Upon returning home in May or June of that year, prior to his departure to take up the ministry in New York, Edwards related the account of his conversion to his father (Murray 1987, 33-35; Winslow [1940] 1979, 90).

> Not long after I first began to experience these things, I gave an account to my father of some things that had passed in my mind. I was pretty much affected by the discourse we had together; and when the discourse was ended, I walked abroad alone, in a solitary place, in my father's pasture, for contemplation. And as I was walking there, and looking upon the sky and clouds, there came into my mind so sweet a sense of the glorious *majesty* and *grace* of God, as I know not how to express.--I seemed to see them both in a sweet conjunction; majesty and meekness joined together: it was a sweet, and gentle, and holy majesty; and also a majestic meekness; an awful sweetness; a high, and great, and holy gentleness (1879, vol. 1, p. lv).

Profile of the Last Puritan

Edwards continued,

> After this my ... gradually increased,
> and became ... more of that
> inward s... g was altered;
> there ... eet cast or
> a... . . I often
> ... he day,
> ... d the
> ... ing
> ...
> ... 1,
> p. ...

[Sticky note annotation:]
Brand "My mind was greatly fixed on divine things, almost perpetually in the contemplation of them. I spent most of my time in thinking of divine things year after year, often walking alone in the woods, + solitary places, for meditation, prayer, + converse with + soliloquy."

The beati... assing phenomenon, but rather an ongoing ... ty, evidenced by his own testimony.

> I felt then grea... tion as to my good estate; but that did not content me. . had vehement longings of soul after God and Christ, and after more holiness. . . . My mind was greatly fixed on divine things; almost perpetually in the contemplation of them. I spent most of my time in thinking of divine things year after year; often walking alone in the woods, and solitary places, for meditation, soliloquy, and prayer, and converse with God: and it was always my manner, at such times, to sing forth my contemplations. I was almost constantly in ejaculatory prayer wherever I was (1879, vol. 1, p. lv).

Edwards's spiritual contemplation of the beatific was progressive, but never self-inflating. Indeed he indicated that he later had to learn his own "extreme feebleness and impotence" and the "bottomless depths of secret corruption and deceit" that were yet within his heart (1879, vol. 1, p. lvi).

Chapter 1

Sometime during 1722-23 Edwards wrote a series of personal "Resolutions." The first one was:

> *Resolved*, That *I will do whatsoever* I think to be most to the glory of God, and my own good, profit, and pleasure, in the whole of my duration; without any consideration of the time, whether now, or never so many myriads of ages hence;

and the last, "Let there be something of benevolence in all that I speak" (1879, vol 1, pp. lxii, lxiv).

While at New York, Edwards would frequently retire to the banks of the Hudson to pray and contemplate. His contemplations of Heaven were noteworthy.

> The heaven I desired was a heaven of holiness; to be with God, and to spend my eternity in divine love, and holy communion with Christ. . . . Heaven appeared exceedingly delightful, as a world of love; and that all happiness consisted in living in pure, humble, heavenly, divine love (1879, vol. 1, p. lvi).

Sereno Dwight, Edwards's great-grandson and biographer, reflected on Edwards's personal account of his conversion, and commented that it was in those early years of Edwards's life that "those correct views were formed which afterwards expanded in his admirable treatise on Religious Affections" (Murray 1987, 482; Edwards 1879, vol. 1, p. lvii).

Edwards left New York in April, 1723, and returned to East Windsor for several months, turned down a call to the pastorate of the Bolton Congregation, and then returned to Yale in June, 1724, having been elected as a tutor. Yale had undergone another radical leadership change with the defection to Anglicanism of Timothy Cutler and Daniel Brown, as well as two neighboring pastors (including Samuel Johnson). Thereafter, adherence to the Saybrook Confession was required for those who held office at Yale. No tolerance for Arminian or prelatical views would be granted (Murray 1987, 53-61).

Thomas Schafer's scholarship has corrected Sereno Dwight's error, perpetuated by Perry Miller and others (Miller [1949] 1973, 52; Winslow [1940] 1979, 60-61), by identifying the period of Edwards's tutorship at Yale (rather than his early collegiate days) as the time when Edwards first read John Locke's *Essay on Human Understanding* and began his "Notes on the Mind" (Anderson 1980).

> It appears that it was also toward the end of 1723 that Edwards began a new notebook, headed "The Mind." The occasion of its origin has been pin-pointed by Thomas Schafer who noted that Edwards, having written an item on "Excellency" in his "Miscellanies" then crossed it out and made the same item a first entry in this new notebook, the contents of which were to be more philosophical than theological. Work on this notebook was pursued during his tutorship, with such entries as, "Place of Minds," "Space," "Thought," "Existence." It is in this manuscript that Edwards's first reference to the English philosopher John Locke occurs (Murray 1987, 64).

Edwards's tutorship at Yale was interrupted by a severe illness which nearly took his life. It was followed by a long convalescence. The sickness, according to his own account, was a time in which "God was pleased to visit me again with the sweet influence of his Spirit." Calling to mind words of the Psalmist, Edwards wrote "And when the light of the day came in at the window, it refreshed my soul, from one morning to another. It seemed to be some image of the light of God's glory." This apparently was a welcome experience for Edwards who declared that when he went to New Haven as tutor he had "sunk in religion" his mind being side-tracked from his "eager pursuits after holiness, by some affairs that greatly perplexed and distracted" him (Edwards 1879, vol. 1, p. lxxv).

On August 29, 1726, Edwards received the call to join his aging grandfather, Solomon Stoddard, in pastoring the prestigious Northampton church. Edwards was ordained on February 22, 1727, and married later that year to Sarah Pierrepont, whose father, James Pierrepont had been a pastor of a New Haven congregation from 1685 until his death in 1714. James Pierrepont had had a prominent role in the founding of Yale College (Murray 1987, 81, 91). In 1723, when he was twenty and Sarah thirteen, Edwards had written for his own amusement the following description of Sarah on the leaf of one of his student books:

> They say there is a young lady in New Haven who is beloved
> of that Great Being who made and rules the world, and that
> there are certain seasons in which this Great Being, in some
> way or other invisible, comes to her and fills her mind with
> exceeding sweet delight, and that she hardly cares for
> anything, except to meditate on him--that she expects after a
> while to be received up where he is, to be raised up out of the
> world and caught up into heaven; being assured that he loves
> her too well to let her remain at a distance from him always.
> There she is to dwell with him, and to be ravished with his
> love and delight for ever. Therefore, if you present all the
> world before her, with the richest of its treasures, she
> disregards it and cares not for it, and is unmindful of any pain
> or affliction. She has a strange sweetness in her mind, and
> singular purity in her affections; is most just and conscientious
> in all her conduct, and you could not persuade her to do
> anything wrong or sinful, if you would give her the whole
> world, lest she should offend this Great Being. She is of a
> wonderful sweetness, calmness and universal benevolence of
> mind; specially after this great God has manifested himself to
> her mind. She will sometimes go about from place to place,
> singing sweetly; and seems to be always full of joy and
> pleasure; and no one knows for what. She loves to be alone,
> walking in the fields and groves, and seems to have some one
> invisible always conversing with her (Murray 1987, 92).

This description of Sarah Pierrepont not only demonstrated Edwards's philosophical bent, but represented Edwards's understanding of the nature of "benevolence" as fittingly rooted, first and foremost in the worth and glory of the Divine Being. The sanctified aesthetic sense of Edwards the philosopher, with all due regard for proper proportion, portrayed Sarah's "greatest share of virtuous benevolence" as directed toward the "one who has the greatest share of universal existence." "True virtue must chiefly consist in love to God; the Being of beings, infinitely the greatest and best" whose Being embraces the welfare of the world (Edwards 1879, 1:125).

> In God, the love of himself and the love of the public are not
> to be distinguished, as in man: because God's being, as it
> were, comprehends all (Edwards 1879, 1:104).

For Edwards, Sarah Pierrepont mirrored that spiritual dawning of the beatific which he himself had experienced and which necessarily led to "universal benevolence of mind." Furthermore, Sarah's beholding of the beatific was cast in the language of the moral philosophers with whose writings Edwards was so familiar.

Edwards was to assist Solomon Stoddard until Stoddard's death in February, 1729 (Murray 1987, 93-94). Thereafter he would continue in the Northampton pastorate until 1750. During that period Jonathan and Sarah Edwards would become parents to eleven children, would open their home to the likes of Samuel Buell, Samuel Hopkins, George Whitefield, and David Brainerd (who would die in their home), would witness the revival fires of the Great Awakening (beginning in their own parish), and eventually would see their own congregation become so resistant to pastoral leadership that Mr. Edwards would be dismissed (Dodds [1971] 1976; Murray 1987, 115-35, 160, 171-72, 179, 300-305, 353-70).

Edwards wrote of a personal event, beatific in nature, which took place three years after the 1734 revival at Northampton. Having ridden his horse into the woods and retired to a secluded spot to pray,

> I had a view, that for me was extraordinary, of the glory of the Son of God, as Mediator between God and man, and his wonderful, great, full, pure, and sweet grace and love, and meek and gentle condescension. This grace that appeared so calm and sweet, appeared also great above the heavens. The person of Christ appeared ineffably excellent.

Of other occasions Edwards would write,

> I have loved the doctrines of the gospel; they have been to my soul like green pastures.
> It has often appeared to me delightful, to be united with Christ; to have him for my Head, and to be a member of his body; also to have Christ for my Teacher and Prophet.
> Sometimes, only mentioning a single word caused my heart to burn within me; or only seeing the name of Christ, or the name of some attribute of God. And God has appeared glorious to me, on account of the Trinity. It has made me have exalting thoughts of God, that he subsists in three persons: Father, Son, and Holy Ghost (1879, vol. 1, p. lxxxix).

It must have been a beatific vision, such as described above, that provided the "heat" and "light" to ignite the Great Awakening fires

(Edwards 1879, 1:243, 281-82). Such a state of spiritual blessedness and "sense" of God's glory provided sufficient moral strength in Edwards so that he would not betray his God, though offered the world. He knew that if church membership were to have any significance it had to be re-established on the basis of the "narrative of grace." The Puritan vision of the city set upon a hill could never be fulfilled corporately unless the church repudiated the compromising admission practices of Stoddardism, as well as the Half-Way Covenant (Morgan [1963] 1982, 151-52; Cherry [1966] 1974, 204; Edwards 1879, 1:443-47).

In order for a corporate image of the beatific to be established via church membership, more than mere doctrinal consent and outward morality was required. Doctrinal consent and outward morality, apart from regeneration, represented nothing more than a "secondary beauty." The "narrative of grace" was essential to the church covenant, for it attested to the experience of regeneration --the foundation of "primary beauty," i.e., "the beauty of holiness." Edwards's "holy taste" could not be satisfied with a beauty that was only of a "secondary" nature, especially when it came to the matter of admission to the Lord's Table. The Northampton congregation opted for the "secondary beauty" of mere doctrinal consent and outward morality (Edwards 1879, 1:127-30, 281-88; 447-49). Ola Winslow wrote, "The warring brethren may have entertained sudden doubts as to their various procedures when, coincident with his departure, the church was struck by lightning and the steeple damaged" ([1940] 1979, 265-66).

Following his dismissal Edwards continued to preach frequently at the Northampton church by the supply committee's request for nearly a year before accepting a call to Stockbridge to minister to the Housatonic Indians. In January, 1758, Edwards set out to accept the call to become president of the College of New Jersey. He died from a smallpox inoculation on March 22, 1758, shortly upon taking office (Winslow [1940] 1979, 261, 265-66, 268-86; Murray 1987, 440-41).

Edwards's legacy included volumes of pastoral, theological, and philosophical writings. His *Narrative of the Surprising Work of God* documented the 1734 revival at Northampton and beyond, and bore the marks of a social scientist, for in it Edwards described, with detached objectivity, the events in which he so passionately played a part. The *Treatise concerning Religious Affections*, described by Dr. Samuel T.

Logan, Jr. as "the most important religious work ever written in America" (1984), was both a defense of spiritual awakening as well as a corrective for many human excesses associated with the Great Awakening in New England. Perry Miller gratuitously spoke of Edwards in reference to his *Religious Affections*: "It would have taken him about an hour's reading in William James and two hours in Freud, to catch up completely" ([1949] 1973, 183). Ola Winslow wrote, "By applying himself to the 'root' of the matter, as his mind demanded, he had made revivals theologically possible" ([1940] 1979, 214). A *History of the Work of Redemption* prompted Miller to say that Edwards "wrote the first truly historical interpretation in American literature," "*a pioneer work* in American historiography," and again, sardonically, "a cosmic rationalization of the communal revival" ([1949] 1973, 311, 314, 315).

During the Stockbridge period Edwards wrote *A Careful and Strict Inquiry into the Prevailing Notions of the Freedom of the Will* (1754) which historian Sydney Ahlstrom described as "one of the literary sensations of eighteenth-century America" (1972, 305). Concerning this masterpiece of logic, Ola Winslow wrote:

> His refutation of the Arminian position amounts, in essence, to a new definition of human liberty by which he thought at one stroke to save both the dignity of man and the omnipotence of God. He grants man freedom of action to carry out his own choices, but insists that those choices are determined by motives, which lie outside of man's control ([1940] 1979, 299).

During the Stockbridge period he wrote *The Great Doctrine of Original Sin Defended*, a rebuttal of John Taylor's Arminianism. Edwards's *Original Sin* would be heralded a century later as among the church's most prized, enduring possessions (Murray 1987, xxiii), indeed "the ablest explication of the Calvinist doctrine on this point ever written" (Edwards 1879, vol. I, p. xl). The *Dissertation on the Nature of True Virtue* was mentioned in the conclusion to *Original Sin*, and was actually written four years prior to that treatise, but was to be published posthumously along with the *Dissertation on the End for Which God Created the World*. Winslow viewed *True Virtue* as a "kind of sequel to the *Religious Affections*"; Ahlstrom, as "clarifying the 'Twelfth Sign' of holy affections" (Winslow [1940] 1979, 308; Ahlstrom 1972, 308-309; Murray 1987, 427-29).

Concerning *True Virtue* and the *End for Which God Created the World*, Murray wrote,

> It is true that, in essence, he is saying nothing more than he taught the Indian children on "man's chief end" from the first question of the Shorter Catechism, but his mind here soars like an eagle towards the sun and of all the experiences which Hopkins and Bellamy enjoyed with their friend there can have been few to equal that winter's day at Stockbridge in 1755 when they heard "Mr. Edwards read a treatise upon the *Last End of God in Creation*" (1987, 428).

Wilbert L. Anderson spoke of Edwards in the following terms:

> This poet-theologian has a habit of ecstasy. He is a Dante never far from the heights of beatific vision. . . . What Edwards beheld as a poet he declared as a preacher. The unity of his spirit and work was complete. Such was his concern for the glory of God and the salvation of men that he used his visions as seer to move the congregations to which he preached (Manspeaker 1981, 9).

Clarence Darrow of the Scopes Trial fame came to a different assessment of Edwards's life.

> "The amazing thing to me," exclaims Darrow, "is why anyone of this generation or any other should *want* to be traced to Jonathan Edwards. Why should an eugenist resort to the devious ways that have been used . . . for the purpose of linking even his worst enemies to Jonathan? Who was Jonathan Edwards? Except for his wierd and horrible theology, he would have filled no place in American life. His main business was scaring silly women and children and blaspheming the God he professed to adore. Nothing but a distorted or diseased mind could have produced his *Sinners in the Hands of an Angry God* (Manspeaker 1981, 48).

John Gerstner appropriately responded to those, such as Darrow, who have accused Edwards of sadistic tendencies for his preaching on the doctrine of eternal punishment: "This is not the spirit of sadism.

Ironically, if Edwards, believing as he did, had been a sadist, he would never have said a word about perdition" (Bogue 1975, 28).

The Philosophical Perspective

Tertullian, at the end of the second century, spurned philosophy with his famous rhetorical question: "What is there in common between Athens and Jerusalem? What between the Academy and the Church?" (Bettenson [1943] 1963, 8). The question of the relationship between the Christian faith and philosophy, revelation and reason, was an issue with which the church had long struggled. The Puritan answer to that question was one of the major themes of Perry Miller's *New England Mind: The Seventeenth Century*. Miller contended that the seeds of philosophy were sown in Puritanism by the adoption of Ramist logic into the systems of Puritan leaders such as Alexander Richardson and William Ames. Petrus Ramus, a sixteenth-century French Protestant philosopher, had posited an objective and coherent system of reality in the universe that was accessible via principles of logic. The key concept, known as "technologia," meant that every discipline was to be defined and classified until the entire system was laid out in a dichotomized scheme of indivisible entities (Miller [1939] 1982, 119, 127, 151, 155; Ames [1629] 1983, 72-73).

> The foundation of technologia was clearly the doctrine that in the mind of God there exists a coherent and rational scheme of ideas upon which He modeled the world (Miller [1939] 1982, 166).

The Puritan adaptation of Ramist principles of logic, according to Perry Miller, was not a metaphysical flight (indeed Ames did not allow a place for metaphysics in his system), but rather a philosophy of the liberal arts showing their unity and interrelationships (Miller [1939] 1982, 160-61; Ames [1629] 1983, 77-78).

> Thus Puritans could appropriate Ramus' *Dialecticae* only on condition that they also appropriate Richardson's preface to it, and "technologia," formulated by him to supply the philosophical apparatus for the unification of Puritanism and logic, systematized by Ames, taught at Harvard, defended in the theses, and expounded in all sermons along with theology,

even as a part of the theology--this is the true metaphysic of Puritanism and the chief tie between its piety and its intellect. As the links must be joined together to make a chain, said Richardson, "so the Arts must be holden together, before there be *Encuclopaidia*." Perhaps we have laid bare the innermost essence of the Puritan mind when we find that its highest philosophical reach was a systematic delineation of the liberal arts (Miller [1939] 1982, 161).

Though Ames, who in many respects was the architect of Puritan thought, would eschew metaphysics and moral philosophy in deference to what he regarded as Christian piety, Fiering pointed out that Edwards "tried to have it both ways" (1981a, 49). A reading of Edwards's treatise on *The Freedom of the Will* reveals the extent of his metaphysical endeavors. Edwards himself certainly acknowledged that the defense of the Calvinistic doctrine that he had set forth would be subject to criticism on the ground that he was engaging in "metaphysics."

> If any should find fault with this reasoning, that it is going a great length into metaphysical niceties and subtilties; I answer, the objection to which they are a reply, is a metaphysical subtilty, and must be treated according to the nature of it (Edwards 1879, 1:74).

> If the reasoning be good, it is as frivolous to inquire what science it is properly reduced to, as what language it is delivered in: and for a man to go about to confute the arguments of his opponent, by telling him, his arguments are *metaphysical*, would be as weak as to tell him, his arguments could not be substantial, because they were written in *French* or *Latin* (Edwards 1879, 1:85).

Fiering stated that Edwards, rather than shunning secular philosophy, "was willing to contend on fine points with the naturalistic moral philosophers of his day" (1981a, 49). Edwards did not despise the "new learning" that had been revived in Europe at the time of the Reformation. Indeed he preferred it to the "barbarous ignorance" that had prevailed in the days of "popery."

> Learning has increased more and more, and at this day is undoubtedly raised to a vastly greater height than ever it was before: and though no good use is made of it by the greater

> part of learned men, yet the increase of learning in itself is a thing to be rejoiced in, because it is a good, and, if duly applied, an excellent handmaid to divinity (Edwards 1879, 1:601).

Edwards spoke of "the great advancement in learning and philosophic knowledge" of the seventeenth and eighteenth centuries as "affording great advantage for a proper and enlarged exercise of our rational powers, and for seeing the bright manifestation of God's perfection in his works" (1879, 1:166).

In order for philosophy to be a useful "handmaid to divinity," however, it was necessary, in Edwards's view to subordinate it to the divine revelation of Holy Scripture. The certainty with which Edwards held to that principle was illustrated in the following statement taken from *A History of the Work of Redemption*:

> And when the gospel came to prevail first without the help of man's wisdom, then God was pleased to make use of learning as a handmaid. So now, learning is at a great height in the world, far beyond what it was in the age when Christ appeared; and now the world by their learning and wisdom, do not know God; and they seem to wander in darkness, are miserably deluded, stumble and fall in matters of religion, as in midnight darkness. Trusting to their learning, they grope in the day-time as in the night. Learned men are exceedingly divided in their opinions concerning the matters of religion, running into all manner of corrupt opinions, pernicious and foolish errors. They scorn to submit their reason to divine revelation, to believe any thing that is above their comprehension; and so being wise in their own eyes, they become fools (Edwards 1879, 1:601).

Edwards looked forward to the day

> when God has sufficiently shown men the insufficiency of human wisdom and learning for the purposes of religion, and when the appointed time comes for that glorious outpouring of the Spirit of God, when he will himself by his own immediate influence enlighten men's minds; then may we hope that God will make use of the great increase of learning as a handmaid of religion, as a means of the glorious advancement of the kingdom of his Son. Then shall human learning be subservient to the understanding of the Scriptures,

and to a clear explanation and a glorious defence of the
doctrines of Christianity (Edwards 1879, 1:601).

Edwards would, on the one hand, marshal a tightly-knit concatenation of philosophical arguments to prepare the way for the scriptural doctrine of the glory of God and, on the other hand, declare that the glory of God itself was self-authenticating so as to render human arguments non-essential in at least ninety-five per cent of cases (Edwards 1879, 1:97-106, 141, 292).

> Thus a soul may have a kind of intuitive knowledge of the divinity of the things exhibited in the gospel; not that he judges the doctrines of the gospel to be from God, without any argument or deduction at all; but it is without any long chain of arguments; the argument is but one, and the evidence direct; the mind ascends to the truth of the gospel but by one step, and that is its divine glory (Edwards 1879, 1:290).

For Edwards the intellect was always involved in the experience of regeneration. Faith involved both understanding and will. Regeneration was not "heat without light." Edwards, however, minimized the role of the speculative aspect of the intellect as being of relatively little importance in the process of conversion.

> He that has doctrinal knowledge and speculation only, without affection, never is *engaged* in the business of religion (1879, 1:238).

> As on the one hand, there must be light in the understanding, as well as an *affected* fervent heart; or where there is heat without light, there can be nothing divine or heavenly in the heart: so, on the other hand, where there is a kind of light without heat, a head stored with notions and speculations with a cold and unaffected heart, there can be nothing divine in that light, that knowledge is no true spiritual knowledge of divine things. If the great things of religion are rightly understood, they will affect the heart (1879, 1:243).

> Not *every* thing that may be called a beauty of *mind*, is properly called virtue. There is a beauty of understanding and speculation; there is something in the ideas and conceptions of great philosophers and statesmen, that may be called beautiful, which is a different thing from what is most commonly meant by virtue.

> But virtue is the beauty of those qualities and acts of the mind, that are of a *moral* nature. . . . Things of this sort . . . do not belong merely to speculation; but to the *disposition* and *will*, or . . . to the *heart* (1879, 1:122).

Though Edwards had a special interest and remarkable aptitude in philosophy as his "Notes on the Mind" attest, and though he would go beyond the point where men such as William Ames were willing to go in debating the great philosophical issues of the day, it was quite apparent that for Edwards philosophy was subordinate to Scripture, reason to revelation, and human wisdom to divine glory.

Edwards's outlook on philosophy was summed up in the following statement in *The Nature of True Virtue*:

> Hence it appears, that those *schemes* of religion or moral philosophy, which--however well in some respects, they may treat of benevolence to *mankind*, and other virtues depending on it, yet--have not a supreme regard to God, and love to him, laid as the *foundation*, and all other virtues handled in *connexion* with this, and in subordination to it, are not true schemes of philosophy, but are fundamentally, and essentially defective (1879, 1:127).

It may be seen from the foregoing that, for Edwards, the overriding issue in any system of thought was the glory of God, and that this was not primarily a philosophical matter, but rather a spiritual matter. It may further be observed that Edwards was primarily a theologian and only secondarily a philosopher. Indeed he engaged in philosophical endeavors, but always with a theological purpose in mind. Carl Bogue was right when he insisted that, for Edwards, theology was the "queen of the sciences" (1975, 35-51). It might also be argued that Edwards was a pastor, primarily, and only secondarily a theologian, for in the final analysis, Edwards's definition of theology was not significantly different from that of William Ames: "Theology is the doctrine or teaching . . . of living to God" (Ames [1629] 1983, 77). Only a failure to appreciate the primacy of the glory of God in Edwards's life could excuse such a condescending appraisal of the Puritan pastor-theologian as that offered by one Georges Lyon:

Chapter 1

There are few names in the eighteenth century which have obtained such celebrity as that of Jonathan Edwards. Critics and historians down to our own day have praised in dithyrambic terms the logical vigor and the constructive powers of a writer whom they hold . . . to be the greatest metaphysician America has yet produced. Who knows, they have asked themselves, to what height, this original genius might have risen, if, instead of being born in a half-savage country, far from the traditions of philosophy and science, he had appeared rather in the old world, and there received the direct impulse of the modern mind. Perhaps he would have taken a place between Leibniz and Kant among the founders of immortal systems, instead of the work he has left, reducing itself to a sublime and barbarous theology, which astonishes our reason and outrages our heart, the object at once of our horror and admiration (Manspeaker 1981, 118-19).

CHAPTER II

MORAL PHILOSOPHY AND THE BENEVOLIST SCHOOL

Pietistic Backgrounds of Benevolism

> Edwards's dissertation on the *Nature of True Virtue* was undoubtedly the best work in moral philosophy written by an American in the eighteenth century. Its appearance was not an anomaly but an altogether expectable event in an era dominated by the special concerns of moral philosophy (Fiering 1981b, 300).

The above statement by Norman Fiering stands as a response to a common misconception that Edwards's *Nature of True Virtue* was an oddity, somewhat out of character with his writings as a whole, or that this work somehow introduced "peculiarities and speculations" into a theology that was otherwise orthodox (Murray 1987, 451-53). Fiering's statement urges us to understand Edwards's *Nature of True Virtue* contextually in order to appreciate it theologically.

That Edwards did not write in a vacuum but addressed issues of his day has generally been recognized with respect to Arminianism and antinomianism, as well as to the matter of his striking middle ground between the rationalism of Charles Chauncy and the "enthusiasm" of James Davenport in the *Religious Affections* (Miller [1949] 1973,

177-96). Edwards's debate with the moral philosophers, however, has only recently been given extensive treatment through the writings of Norman Fiering. Fiering cited the emergence of moral philosophy as an "autonomous, naturalistic introspective science of human nature" during the last quarter of the seventeenth century as the philosophical background for Edwards's *Nature of True Virtue* and others of his writings as well (1981b, 10-62, 295; 1981a, 1-8). Fiering connected the rise of moral philosophy to the gradual disintegration of the scholastic, intellectualist, ethical system based on Aristotle's *Nicomachean Ethics*, and its replacement by an ethical system rooted in human sentiment or the affections (1981b, 5-6).

> The new moral philosophy was also characterized by sophisticated and innovated analyses of conscience and obligation, by a preoccupation with the moral criterion of benevolence (a criterion foreign to Classical and Scholastic ethics), and by a notable admixture of moral exhortation that made the subject more than merely academic. . . . The "new moral philosophy," in other words, combined descriptive and prescriptive ethics to a degree seldom attempted in the twentieth century (Fiering 1981a, 6).

T. A. Roberts stated that the eighteenth-century philosophical world

> adopted a view concerning the motivation of human actions, and in particular of moral actions . . . that human actions, in the sense of deliberate, intentional actions, are always motivated by some desire or inclination, and that in the absence of any such desire or inclination, any rational recognition or awareness of what is to be done is impotent to motivate action. There are several affections or feelings which can motivate action, but self-love and benevolence are the most important (1973, 107-108).

In describing the shift from an "intellectualist" to a "sentimentalist" approach to ethics, Fiering was careful to point out that such a transition did not represent the total rejection of rationalism. On the contrary,

> there was a continuous tradition of rationalist theology in New England, a tradition that certainly did not exclude piety and devotionalism, although it did eschew fideism or any suggestion that God is altogether unintelligible. To be more specific, two kinds of rationalism vied for authority in the early seventeenth century, the Aristotelian Scholastic and the Platonist, the latter of which is evident in Richardson. With the universal repudiation of Scholasticism after mid-century, Platonism expanded to fill the vacuum in metaphysics left by the disintegration of the Aristotelian synthesis (1981b, 251).

Fiering went on to say that

> Platonism had the virtue . . . of being historically compatible with affectional religion, even with mysticism, which made it quite congruous with existing tendencies in New England religion (1981b, 251).

It was ironic that the eminent Puritan leader William Ames had "unwittingly" contributed to the rise of the new moral philosophy as an "autonomous" discipline (Fiering 1981b, 44). Ames himself had soundly rejected moral philosophy as an "autonomous" discipline divorced from the study of theology.

> But as with the standard of well-doing so it is with the standard of virtue, namely, that the sole rule in all matters which have to do with the direction of life is the revealed will of God (Ames [1629] 1983, 225; Fiering 1981b, 24-25).

But in rejecting an autonomous system of ethics, Ames had also firmly rejected Aristotle and his ethics based on rational deliberation.

> Aristotle holds to the Lesbian or crooked law that the judgment of prudent men is the rule for virtue. But there are nowhere such wise men under whose judgment we might stand and, even if there were, they could not always be known or consulted by the would-be virtuous. . . .
> 15. What is called right reason, if it is to lead to absolute rectitude, is nowhere else to be discovered than where it is--in the Scriptures. It does not differ from the will of God

> revealed for the direction of our life (Ps. 119:66). *Teach me the excellency of reason and knowledge for I believe your precepts.* When the imperfect notions about honesty and dishonesty found in man's mind after the fall are truly understood, they will be seen to be incapable of shaping virtue. They do not differ a whit from the written law of God except that they are imperfect and obscure.
>
> 16. Therefore, there can be no other teaching of the virtues than theology which brings the whole revealed will of God to the directing of our reason, will, and life (Ames [1629] 1983, 225-26; Fiering 1981b, 71-72).

Fiering pointed out that Ames made theology a "part" of a larger system of the "Arts" and that, through Richardson's influence, Ames bought into a system of "practical theology" which made theology the "art of living" (an insidious vestige of Aristotelianism). This emphasis "coincided with an existing trend in academic philosophy" and "gave great impetus to the growth of the new moral philosophy." What followed was the "gradual absorption of seventeenth-century pietism into a philosophical movement, namely, moral enthusiasm or virtue devotion" (1981b, 26, 44-51).

William Ames's pietistic approach to ethics had its roots in Augustinian pietism, or voluntarism, which emphasized the importance of the will, as distinct from the Aristotelian intellect--notwithstanding Perry Miller's erroneous statement contrariwise (Fiering 1981b, 121, 125-26; Miller [1939] 1982, 3-34, 248). Indeed many of the issues of moral philosophy raised in the seventeenth century, and which would subsequently be addressed in the writings of Jonathan Edwards, were anticipated by Augustine.

The encounter with Neoplatonism, which pointed to God as the source of all good and reality, had been a significant step toward Augustine's conversion (Walker [1918] 1959, 161). Augustine's piety was subsequently expressed in his *City of God* in terms which gave a significant role to the emotions.

> The "citizens of the holy City of God feel fear and desire, pain and gladness while they live in God's fashion during the pilgrimage of their present existence, and because their love is right, all these feelings of theirs are right" (Fiering 1981b, 152).

The voluntarist nature of Augustine's moral philosophy, with its regard for emotions, was further evident in the following passage from the *City of God*:

> Man's will, then, is all-important. If it is badly directed, the emotions will be perverse; if it is rightly directed, the emotions will not be merely blameless but even praiseworthy. The will is in all of these affections; indeed, they are nothing else but inclinations of the will. For, what are desire and joy but the will in harmony with things we desire? And what are fear and sadness but the will in disagreement with things we abhor? (1958, 303)

Augustine continued,

> The consent of the will in the search for what we want is called desire; joy is the name of the will's consent to the enjoyment of what we desire. So, too, fear is aversion from what we do not wish to happen, as sadness is a disagreement of the will with something that happened against our will. Thus, according as the will of a man is attracted or repelled by the variety of things which he either seeks or shuns, so is it changed or converted into one or other of these different emotions (1958, 304).

Matters such as "self-love" and "happiness" which were to become such central issues in Jonathan Edwards's debate with the moral philosophers had been practically thematic for Augustine whose "eudaemonism" has met with some objection (O'Donovan 1980, 142).

> For He is the source of our happiness and the very end of all our aspirations. . . . We pursue Him with our love so that when we reach Him we may rest in perfect happiness in Him who is our goal. For our goal (or, as the philosophers in their endless disputes have termed it, our end or good) is nothing else than union with Him whose spiritual embrace, if I may so speak, can alone fecundate the intellectual soul and fill it with virtue.
>
> It is this Good which we are commanded to love with our whole heart, with our whole mind, and with all our strength. It is toward this Good that we should be led by those who love us, and toward this Good we should lead those whom we love.

After citing the two great commandments, Augustine continued,

> For, in order that a man might learn how to love himself, a standard was set to regulate all his actions on which his happiness depends. For, to love one's own self is nothing but to wish to be happy, and the standard is union with God. When, therefore, a person who knows how to love himself is bidden to love his neighbor as himself, is he not, in effect, commanded to persuade others, as far as he can, to love God? . . .
>
> It follows, therefore, that if any immortal power, however highly endowed with virtue, loves us as itself, it must wish us to be subject, for our own happiness, to Him in submission to whom it finds its happiness (1958, 191).

O'Donovan defended Augustine's "eudaemonism" as he noted the ontological foundation which underlay Augustinian self-love.

> In coupling self-love (benevolence) with the cosmic love of God, Augustine . . . asserted God's ontological position as the source of all good and beatitude--in case anybody should be so foolish as to suppose he could be altruistic toward God (1980, 40).

For Augustine, there was no virtue of self-love that was independent of the love of God and, conversely, no love of God that could be totally unrelated to self-love. It was also noteworthy, in view of Edwards's later doctrine, that Augustine regarded the Holy Spirit as the "self-love" of the Godhead or the mutual love that co-existed between the Father and the Son (O'Donovan 1980, 37, 128-129, 134-35; Edwards 1879, 1:126; Gerstner 1987, 32-34).

Ulrich Zwingli, the Rhineland Reformer, in seeming contradiction to Augustine, would later regard self-love as the root problem of sin rather than projecting it as an acceptable ethical motive. Zwingli viewed regeneration as God's ignition of a fire in the heart "by which to kindle love of Him in place of ourselves; and He desires this fire to burn" ([1929] 76, 78, 81, 84, 86-87, 141).

John Calvin, the Geneva Reformer, similarly, did not ascribe any virtue to self-love.

> In the entire law we do not read one syllable that lays a rule upon man as regards those things which he may or may

> not do, for the advantage of his own flesh. And obviously, since men were born in such a state that they are all too much inclined to self-love--and, however much they deviate from the truth, they still keep self-love--there was no need of a law that would increase or . . . enkindle. . . . Hence it is very clear that we keep the commandment not by loving ourselves but by loving God and neighbor. . . .
>
> Indeed, to express how profoundly we must be inclined to love our neighbors [Lev 19:18], the Lord measured it by the love of ourselves because he had at hand no more violent or stronger emotion than this. . . . He does not concede the first place to self-love ["Φιλαυτια," according to the footnote] as certain Sophists stupidly imagine, and assign the second place to love (1960, 1:417-18).

Thus, by way of summary, Ames's voluntarism, with its roots in Augustinian piety, lent itself unwittingly to the seventeenth-century emergence of an autonomous, introspective moral philosophy rooted in human sentiment. Whereas Reformers, Zwingli and Calvin, had abstained, William Ames evidently imbibed the Augustinian wine of self-love reasoning as follows:

> Since our love is a desire of union with God it comes in part from what is called concupiscence or appetite. We desire God for ourselves, because we hope for benefit and eternal blessedness from him.

Ames immediately added, however, "The highest end of this love should be God himself" ([1629] 1983, 251).

The Cartesian Revolution

Though the Augustinian pietistic influence via William Ames would be a contributing factor in the emergence of the new moral philosophy, Descartes and those who followed would make the significant impact.

> The great strides in the modern interpretation of the passions did not begin until Descartes's treatise on the subject was published at mid-century, followed by the basic work of Nicolas Malebranche, and then by the essays of the third earl of Shaftesbury, his disciple Francis Hutcheson, and the other Scottish moralists (Fiering 1981b, 178).

Descartes subjected scholastic and classical ideas to the test of critical reason and also stressed the importance of empirical observation of human nature.

Nicolas Malebranche (1638-1715), a disciple of Descartes, greatly influenced John Locke, Bishop Berkeley and the Third Earl of Shaftesbury, but his public recognition diminished either because of his association with Descartes (eclipsed by Newton), or because of being regarded an "enthusiast" in the matter of religion. Jonathan Edwards's catalogue of reading indicated that he had read some of Malebranche's writing, including *Search After Truth*, and that he probably did so prior to 1726 (Avey [1954] 1961, 138; Fiering 1981a, 40-44; Shaftesbury 1963, vol. I, p. ix).

A scanning of the chapter headings of *Search After Truth* reveals the prominent position given to such topics as "ideas," "sensations," and "inclinations," and serves to establish the late seventeenth-, and early eighteenth-century moral philosophical milieu into which Edwards was born. Malebranche is particularly important for the thesis of this book, however, because some of his key theological concepts foreshadowed those of Jonathan Edwards. Especially significant was that, for Malebranche, God was the "*End*" in the moral philosophical scheme.

> 'Tis an undeniable Truth, that *God can have no other Principal End of his Actions, than Himself*: and that he may have many *Subordinate* Ends, tending to the Preservation of the Beings he has created. He can have no Principal End besides Himself: because, being not liable to error he can [not] place his ultimate End in Beings that include not all of Perfection. . . . *God* therefore *Wills* His *Glory*, as the Principal End; and the Preservation of His *Creatures*, only for His Glory (1700, 138).

In the introduction to his *Dissertation on the End for Which God Created the World*, Edwards discussed "chief ends," "subordinate ends," and "ultimate ends"; and in the body of the dissertation he set forth a Malebranche-type thesis that God makes himself his chief and highest end in all that he does (1879, 1:97-121).

In *Nature of True Virtue* Edwards stated,

> God's goodness and love to created beings, is derived from and subordinate to his love to himself.

He added (as a footnote),

> In what manner it is so, I have endeavoured in some measure to explain in the preceding discourse of *God's end in creating the world* (1879, 1:127).

Malebranche had expressed the same thought fifty years earlier in *Search After Truth*.

> As there is but *One Love* properly in God, that is, the Love of Himself; and as He can love nothing but by that Love, since He can love nothing but with reference to *Himself* (1700, 138).

Malebranche also took up the theme of human self-love stating that there was a proper place assigned to it by God and that such self-love was designed for human self-preservation.

> 'Tis his Will, therefore, that they all have a natural Inclination for their own Preservation, and that they love themselves. So that Self-love is reasonable, because Man is really amiable; in as much as God loves us, and would have us love our selves: but it is not reasonable to love ourselves better than God; since God is infinitely more lovely than we are. It is unjust for us to place our ultimate End in our selves, and to centre our Love there without reference to God; since having no real Goodness, or Subsistence of our selves, but only by the participation of the Goodness and Being of GOD, we are no farther amiable than we stand related to him (1700, 147).

[Margin note: Emerson-like until now]

The bestowal of a kind of natural self-love for the sake of human preservation was an idea which Edwards expounded in *True Virtue* just as he did the idea of loving on the basis of "Goodness" and "Subsistence," when he made the degree of "existence" and "excellence," respectively, the primary and secondary ground of love (1879, 1:125, 135-37). It is almost a certainty, however, that Edwards, who described his own "wickedness" as "infinite upon infinite," could never have used the term "amiable" in reference to man, except in the sense that God saw the reflection of his own effulgence in man (1879, vol. 1, p. xc; 1:100, 120).

Malebranche's understanding of the relationship of self-love to the Fall was also anticipatory of Edwards's doctrine.

> Nevertheless, the Inclination we should have for GOD, is lost by the Fall; and our will now has only an infinite Capacity for all Goods, or Good in general; and a strong Inclination to possess them, which can never be destroyed. But the Inclination which we ought to have for our own Preservation, or *our Self-Love*, is so mightily increas'd, that 'tis at last become the absolute Master of our own Will: It has even chang'd and converted the Love of GOD, or the Inclination we have for Good in general and that due to other Men, into its own nature. For it may be said, that the Love of our selves at present ingrosses all because we Love all things but with relation to our selves (Malebranche 1700, 147).

For Malebranche this love to "Good in general" was "natural" and though its origin was in God, it had become creature-centered as a result of the Fall (1700, 138).

Edwards, in his treatise on *Original Sin*, stated that man was created with "two kinds of principles"--an "*inferior* kind" which was "NATURAL" and oriented toward "self-love," and a "*superior*" principle which was "spiritual." As a result of Adam's sin, "those superior principles had left his heart."

> The inferior principles of self-love, and natural appetite, which were given only to serve, being alone, and left to themselves, *of course* became reigning principles; having no superior principles to regulate or control them, they became absolute masters of the heart. . . . Man immediately set up *himself*, and the objects of his private affections and appetites, as supreme; and so they took the place of GOD (1879, 1:217-18).

[Margin note: Emerson might say that Man & nature are God. To be Self-reliant is to be worshiped?]

It was most unfortunate that the major thrust of the new moral philosophy movement did not continue in the theocentric vein in which Malebranche operated. Indeed the Third Earl of Shaftesbury and Francis Hutcheson would turn from those "enthusiastic" aspects of Malebranche and dilute the theological base gravitating toward a more humanitarian emphasis--while, at the same time, forging ahead with the Cartesian principles of critical reason, empirical observation, and skepticism. Before their positions are examined, it is essential to view the writings of Thomas Hobbes and John Locke, inasmuch as the Shaftesbury-Hutcheson gospel of benevolism was really a response to Hobbes, as well as to Locke (Hutcheson [1742] 1969, "Introduction," ix).

Hobbes (1588-1679), in Cartesian style, rejected Aristotelian scholasticism following the premise that the only proper foundation for moral philosophy was observation (Hobbes 1958, viii-ix; Fiering 1981b, 254). Thereby he "forced the questions of ethics onto ground such as had not quite been the case since the time of St. Augustine."

> What Hobbes claimed to have discovered in human nature through his introspective and empirico-deductive method was rather disconcerting: predominantly selfish instincts redeemed only by an ignoble capacity to calculate one's way toward a practical accommodation with others (Fiering 1981b, 255).

The following excerpt from *Leviathan* illustrates how Hobbes founded his ethical norms on the basis of the empirico-deductive method thereby making the descriptive determinative for the prescriptive:

> Moral philosophy is nothing else but the science of what is *good* and *evil* in the conversation and society of mankind. *Good* and *evil* are names that signify our appetites and aversions, which in different tempers, customs, and doctrines of men are different; and different men differ not only in their judgment on the senses of what is pleasant and unpleasant to the taste, smell, hearing, touch and sight but also of what is conformable or disagreeable to reason in the action of common life (1958, 131).

T. A. Roberts said that Hobbes had explained away "compassion" as nothing more than the fear of experiencing the same misery of the person in distress. "Benevolence," for Hobbes, amounted to an action based on the love of power over the life of another (Roberts 1973, 63, 70). For Hobbes, *self-interest* was the underlying motive for all human behavior.

> Whensoever a man transfers his right or renounces it, it is either in consideration of some right reciprocally transfered [*sic*] to himself or for some other good he hopes for thereby.

> For it is a voluntary act; and of the voluntary acts of every man, the object is some *good to himself* (Hobbes 1958, 112).

> The final cause, end or design of men, who naturally love liberty and dominion over others, in the introduction of that restraint upon themselves in which we see them live in commonwealth is the foresight of their own preservation, and of a more contented life thereby (Hobbes 1958, 139).

The benevolist school would sharply differ with Hobbes over the description of human nature. Edwards himself, though he had not read Hobbes's works (Edwards 1879, 1:69), insisted that there were such things as "natural affection," "gratitude," and "pity that amounted to nothing but extensions of self-love." These were expressions of God's common grace for the preservation of human society. They did not consist of true virtue, their beauty being merely of a *secondary* nature (1879, 1:129, 135-39).

John Locke (1632-1704), as Hobbes had done, developed a theory of human government but went further than Hobbes in analyzing the structure of human experience. Locke in his *Essay on Human Understanding* (1690) rejected Descartes's concept of innate ideas insisting instead that the human mind was "white paper" at birth "void of all characters." All "materials of reason and knowledge" were derived from "EXPERIENCE." "SENSATIONS" were the source of most ideas. "SENSATIONS" were followed by "perception"--the mind's operation which was the "internal sense" or "REFLECTIONS" (Avey [1954] 1961, 141-42; Locke 1952, 121-22).

Locke, in rejecting all innate ideas, rejected any innate ideas of morality or native moral sense. Anticipating a challenge to his thesis, Locke argued,

> Perhaps it will be urged, that the tacit assent of their minds agrees to what their practice contradicts. I answer, first, I have always thought the actions of men the best interpreters of their thoughts. But, since it is certain that most men's practices, and some men's open professions, have either questioned or denied these principles, it is impossible to establish a universal consent . . . without which it is impossible to conclude them innate. Secondly, it is very strange and unreasonable to suppose innate practical principles, that terminate only in contemplation. Practical principles derived from nature, are there for operation, and

must produce conformity of action, not barely speculative assent to their truth or else they are in vain distinguished from speculative maxims (1952, 104).

Thus, in defining innate moral ideas, Locke united belief with practice as Edwards was later so careful to do in spelling out the dimensions of the "supernatural spiritual sense" or "holy taste" in *Religious Affections*. Though Edwards would use Lockean language to describe regeneration, would agree that belief and practice ought to be united in the moral sense, and would similarly argue that such a sense was not to be found in the natural man, Edwards's "moral sense" or "sense of the heart" represented a sharp repudiation of Lockean empirical psychology. The "holy taste" was supernaturally imparted to the soul by the Holy Spirit--it was not mediated merely through the physical senses (Edwards 1879, 1:264-74, 281-88, 314-36; Fiering 1981a, 125-26). Edwards would even refer to "a new inward *perception* or *sensation*," "what some metaphysicians call a new *simple idea*," but he was talking about the experience of God's supernatural grace as the context clearly indicates. When Locke used these terms, he was describing his theory of the natural process or structure of human learning distinguishing it from the theory of innateness (Edwards 1879, 1:266; Locke 1952, 121-29).

This radical difference between Locke and Edwards needs to be emphasized, despite Edwards's use of Lockean terminology, because of the gross distortion of Edwards perpetrated by Perry Miller in his biography of Edwards. Miller let his imagination run wildly, depicting Edwards as a sensationist who was thoroughly committed to Lockean principles of empirical psychology (Miller [1949] 1973, 43-68). Fiering acknowledged Edwards's use of Locke's terms but insisted,

> Edwards circumvented Locke by borrowing enough of his fashionable language to satisfy his empiricist critics. But except for the accidental parallel to Lockean simple ideas, such as the taste of honey or the sight of the color red, Edwards's spiritual sense has little resemblance to anything in Locke, and the English philosopher, had he been alive, would undoubtedly have dismissed Edwards's idea of a special sensation of divine things as "enthusiastick" nonsense.

In a footnote Fiering added,

> In *Religious Affections*, ed. Smith, 215-216, Edwards disparaged Locke's sensations as sources of knowledge in much the same fashion as Malebranche disparaged sense impressions: "The external ideas men have are the lowest sort of ideas. These ideas may be raised only by impressions made on the body, by moving the animal spirits, and impressing the brain. . . . These external ideas are as much below the more intellectual exercises of the soul, as the body is a less noble part of man than the soul" (1981a, 125-26).

Edwards did echo a principle which Locke had expounded --that men do by nature seek their own happiness and have an aversion to their own misery. Locke had viewed these human tendencies as "inclinations of the appetite"; Edwards, simply as evidence of the faculty of the will (Locke 1952, 104; Edwards 1879, 1:141).

Locke had dealt with the issue of ethical motive and had misrepresented the Christian position.

> If a Christian who has the view of happiness and misery in another life, be asked why a man must keep his word, he will give this reason:--Because God, who has the power of eternal life and death, requires it of us. But if a Hobbist be asked why? he will answer:--Because the public requires it, and Leviathan will punish you if do not, And if one of the old philosophers had been asked, he would have answered:--Because it was dishonest, below the dignity of man, and opposite to virtue, the highest perfection of human nature, to do otherwise (1952, 105).

Edwards, according to Samuel Hopkins, was to derive more pleasure from Locke's *Essay* "'than the most greedy miser finds when gathering up handfuls of gold'" (Murray 1987, 64). Edwards's pleasure, however, did not keep him from setting the record straight on the true Christian motive.

> *The first objective ground of gracious affections, is the transcendently excellent and amiable nature of divine things, as they are in themselves; and not any conceived relation they bear to self, or self-interest* (1879, 1:274).

Edwards, of course, would also deal with the "Hobbist" ethic and declare that *public benevolence* was generally no more virtuous than an aesthetic appreciation of architectural design and, in the final analysis, amounted to nothing more than self-love (1879, 1:128-29, 131-32). As for moral philosophy rooted in human dignity alone, without primary reference to the glory of God, Edwards would regard it as "fundamentally and essentially defective" (1879, 1:127). Edwards certainly agreed with Locke's thesis that God had "by an inseparable connexion joined virtue and public happiness together," when he stated that "true virtue most essentially consists in BENEVOLENCE TO BEING IN GENERAL" (Locke 1952, 105; Edwards 1879, 1:122). But he set his own thesis apart from Locke's when he spelled out the implications of that statement, concluding,

> From what has been said, it is evident, that true virtue must chiefly consist in LOVE OF GOD; the Being of beings, infinitely the greatest and best (1879, 1:125).
>
> If the Deity is to be looked upon as within that system of beings which properly terminates our benevolence, or belonging to the whole, certainly he is to be regarded as the *head* of the system, and the *chief* part of it: if it be proper to call him a *part*, who is infinitely more than all the rest, and in comparison of whom, and without whom, all the rest are nothing, either as to beauty or existence (1879, 1:126).

Richard Lovelace accurately summed up Locke's influence on Edwards--"more as a storehouse of metaphors than as a theological source" (1985, 19). Perry Miller, to a degree, acknowledged as much in such a statement as the following:

> The simplest, and most precise, definition of Edwards' thought is that it was Puritanism recast in the idiom of empirical psychology ([1949] 1973, 62).

Edwards, however, as Lovelace stated, "would not have attributed the awakening impact of his sermons to any rhetoric of sensation, but to the Spirit's penetration" (1985, 19).

The Benevolist School

Locke had echoed what Hobbes had stated earlier that human nature on the basis of empirical observation was demonstrably rooted in self-interest, and human theories of government were concessions to that empirical fact. The benevolist school of Shaftesbury, Hutcheson, and Hume would challenge that thesis. The philosophical system of Anthony Ashley Cooper, Third Earl of Shaftesbury (1671-1713), contained several propositions that would later become critical issues for Edwards: (1) The universe was governed by a beneficent Mind, and consequently there was no "ill" in the system when considered as a whole; (2) Benevolence was the proper "frame of mind" for man who was so constituted that his happiness was tied to benevolent affections; (3) Faith was of positive value but the lack of it was not a detriment; (4) While evil delight did exist, it was "unnatural"; (5) God was to be loved and obeyed but not on the basis of future reward or punishment--otherwise love and obedience would not constitute virtue; (6) Aesthetics and ethics (the Beautiful and the Good) were inseparably related; consequently bad morals were simply a lack of cultural refinement (Shaftesbury 1963, vol. 1, pp. xxix-xxxi).

Edwards's assertion of the doctrine of eternal punishment as an integral part of his system was his way of clarifying the nature of the God whose holiness was being skirted in the Shaftesbury version of Deity.

> The existence of hell (in the orthodox conception) became a key issue in Edwards's struggle with the sentimental humanitarianism of the age, which led to his formulation of one of the few effective critiques of the ethics of compassion in the eighteenth century (Fiering 1981a, 201).

If Shaftesbury were to bind ethics and aesthetics together, Edwards would respond in kind by defining "true virtue" on biblical grounds as the "beauty of holiness," and affirm, on that basis, the doctrine of hell (1879, 1:279-84; 1:127). For Edwards, the "beauty of holiness" was the primary beauty, and it consisted in "cordial consent" to "being in general," which involved the surrender of one's "infinitely inferior" private interests to the "infinitely superior" interest of the "Being of beings." To direct one's affection to a private system, insubordinate to the Supreme Being--though the system be as vast as the universe--was to set oneself in opposition to "general existence" to an infinite degree, and ultimately to love one's own misery. Punishment, proportional to the offense, would necessarily be infinite in degree and duration. In Edwards's view that constituted hell. Thus to affirm beauty was also to affirm the reality of eternal punishment--notwithstanding the objections of the benevolist school (Edwards 1879, 1:224-38, 628-29, 669-71).

For Edwards, the benevolent "frame of mind" was equated with the "spiritual sense" supernaturally imparted to the soul as a gift of God in regeneration. The issue of relationship between the love of God and self-interest raised by Shaftesbury would become a major focal point of Edwards in his *Treatise concerning Religious Affections* (Edwards 1879, 1:141, 274-78).

Francis Hutcheson (1694-1747), Irish-born son of a Presbyterian minister and Professor of Moral Philosophy at Glasgow University, was considered the "father of Scottish philosophy." He himself was influenced by Shaftesbury and Locke and he was to have a formative influence on David Hume. Hutcheson coined the expression "the greatest good for the greatest number" thus laying the foundation for the utilitarian theory of ethics which would be developed later (Avey [1954] 1961, 158; Hutcheson [1742] 1969, Introduction, x; Roberts 1973, 2-3).

Hutcheson took issue with Locke over the concept of innate senses. He addressed the matter in the preface to his *Essay on the Nature and Conduct of the Passions and Affections*.

> It were to be wished, that those who were at such Pains to prove a beloved Maxim, that "all Ideas arise from *Sensation* and *Reflection*," had so explained themselves, that none should take their meaning to be that all our Ideas are either *external Sensations*, or *reflex Acts* upon *external Sensations*: Or if by *Reflection* they mean an *inward Power of Perception*, as Mr. Locke declares expressly, calling it *internal Sensation*, that they had as carefully examined into the several kinds of *internal Perceptions*, as they have done into the *external Sensations*: That we might have seen whether the former be not as *natural* and *necessary* and *ultimate*, without reference to any others, as the latter ([1742] 1969, x-xi).

Hutcheson objected to Locke and Hobbes who in their attempt to correct the errors of the "Schoolmen" (Aristotelians), had themselves introduced "Confusion, by attempting to take away some of the most immediate *simple Perceptions*," such as "Approbation, Condemnation, Pleasure and Pain" explaining them as related to the "External Senses."

> In like manner they have treated our *Desires* or *Affections*, making the most generous, kind and disinterested of them to proceed from *Self-Love*, by some subtle Trains of Reasoning, to which honest Hearts are often wholly Strangers (Hutcheson [1742] 1969, vii [vi]).

Hutcheson was thus postulating an innate moral sense in men whereby men might and, in his view, did live lives of disinterested benevolence. Hutcheson did not go quite as far as Shaftesbury in regard to disinterested benevolence in that he did not rule out that a person might engage in benevolent action through the influence of reward or punishment; but he did rule out the possibility that gaining private advantage by deliberate intention could co-exist with benevolent action (Roberts 1973, 13). Hutcheson's differences with Shaftesbury may be seen in the following statement:

> The Prospect of any *Interest* may be a Motive to us, to desire whatever we apprehend as the *Means* of obtaining it. Particularly, "if *Rewards* of any kind are proposed to those who have virtuous Affections, this would raise in us the Desire of having these *Affections*, and would incline us to use all the Means to raise them in ourselves; particularly *to turn our Attention* to all the Qualities in the DEITY, or our Fellows, which are naturally apt to raise the virtuous Affections." Thus it is, that Interest of any kind may influence us indirectly to Virtue, and Rewards particularly may over-balance all to Vice. . . .
>
> This may let us see that "the Sanctions of *Rewards* and *Punishments*, as proposed in the Gospel, are not rendered useless or unnecessary, by supposing the virtuous Affections to be disinterested" (Hutcheson [1742] 1969, 25-26).

Hutcheson grouped most of the significant affections under "Love and Hatred." Love toward rational agents was subdivided into "love of complacence, or esteem" and "love of benevolence." Complacence was more properly defined as a *perception* rather than an affection since it was simply the "approbation of a person by the moral sense." Benevolence was an affection defined as "the desire of the happiness of others." The opposites of complacence and benevolence were said to be "dislike" and "malice," respectively (Roberts 1973, 7).

"Love of complacence" and "love of benevolence" were to become foundational concepts in Edwards's *Nature of Virtue*, though he would base his ethical system upon the objective standard of the Godhead rather than upon the tentative conclusions of empirical psychology (Edwards 1879, 1:123-25).

Hutcheson, on the other hand, had even postulated his theology on the basis of empirical psychology. Reasoning inductively from empirical observation of the so-called "Internal Sense," Hutcheson insisted that man could conclude, not only that God existed, but that his nature was "Benevolent" rather than "wrathful" ([1742] 1969, 177-80).

> We may only on this occasion consider the Evidences of divine Goodness appearing in the structure of our own Nature, and in the Order of our Passions and Senses ([1742] 1969, 179).

Hutcheson's ethical system, thus, both glorified human nature and brought God down to the level of human nature, thereby robbing God of his infinite glory. Furthermore, though he insisted on an inner moral sense, he refused to make man accountable to God on the basis of that moral sense.

> If the *Idea of a* DEITY be neither imprinted, nor offer itself previously to any *Reflection,* nor be universally excited by *Tradition*, the bare *Want* of it, where there has been no *Tradition* or *Reflection*, cannot be called criminal upon any Scheme (Hutcheson [1742] 1969, 323).

Hutcheson could scarcely imagine a person unaware of a "governing Mind" and of a "Right and Wrong in Morals," but as to whether this was to be attributed to "*innate* Ideas," "universal tradition," or "some *necessary Determination*" in human nature, his attitude was simply one of indifference--"Let the curious inquire" ([1742] 1969, 324). Hutcheson failed to see any suggestion in man's nature that "virtuous affections" should be "only towards God." According to his thinking, such an idea arose "from the long subtle *Reasonings* of Men at leisure, and unemployed in the natural Affairs of Life" ([1742] 1969, 339).

> If to make a Mind virtuous or even innocent, it be necessary that it should have such sublime Speculations of God, as the $\tau\grave{o}\ \pi\hat{\alpha}\nu$ in the *Intellectual active System* (if we call *one Agent* in many *Passive Organs* an *active System*), then

> God has placed the Bulk of Mankind in an absolute *Incapacity* of Virtue, and inclined them perpetually to infinite Evil, by their very *Instincts* and *natural Affections* ([1742] 1969, 338).

Hutcheson concluded the matter by absolving his ethical scheme from any absolute dependence upon God as a point of reference.

> However we must look upon that Temper as exceedingly *imperfect*, *inconstant*, and *partial*, in which *Gratitude toward the universal Benefactor*, *Admiration* and *Love* of the *Supreme original Beauty*, *Perfection* and *Goodness*, are not the strongest and most *prevalent* Affections; yet *particular Actions* may be innocent, nay, virtuous where there is no actual *Intention* of pleasing the DEITY, influencing the Agent ([1742] 1969, 339).

One can readily see from the above statements that Edwards's challenge went beyond the simple issues of "enthusiasm" and rationalism when he penned his *Treatise concerning Religious Affections*; the theological issues were more complex than the Great Awakening polarity between Davenport and Chauncy (Miller [1949] 1973, 178). Hutcheson and others of the benevolist school had provided the grist and the challenge for theological-philosophical polemics--polemics for purpose of clarification. Jonathan Edwards would see his calling as giving New England Puritanism "a philosophical structure, which would make it rationally credible and more enduring than it could be without the aid of philosophy." Norman Fiering stated,

> In the late seventeenth century moral philosophy had begun the process of converting into secular and naturalistic terms crucial parts of the Christian heritage. Edwards in a sense reversed the ongoing process by assimilating the moral philosophy of his time and converting it back into the language of religious thought and experience (1981a, 60).

Statements such as the following from Edwards's *Religious Affections* take on new meaning when regarded against the background of the Hutchesonian benevolist gospel.

> This holy relish discerns and distinguishes between good and evil, between holy and unholy, without being at the trouble of a train of reasoning (1879, 1:286).

> There is no other *true virtue*, but *real holiness* (1879, 1:279).
>
> The saints' affections begin with *God*; and self-love has a hand in these affections consequently and secondarily only (1879, 1:276).
>
> Truly gracious affections arise from special and peculiar influences of the Spirit, working that *sensible effect* or *sensation* in the souls of the saints, which are entirely different from all that is possible a natural man should experience (1879, 1:267).

Ironically, Edwards would agree with Hutcheson that there was a sense in which God in his sovereignty had "placed the Bulk of Mankind in an absolute *Incapacity* of Virtue." That was indeed the state of unregenerate men. Hutcheson had said it in cynicism. Edwards would affirm it as a theological and empirical reality in *Freedom of the Will* and *Original Sin*. Indeed the Scriptures themselves had affirmed it: "For God has bound all men over to disobedience" (Rom 11:32a NIV). Hutcheson could not see beyond "Nature" and Edwards would state the reason in *Religious Affections*--only grace could enable a man to see. In insisting that men were bound over to "incapacity" or, as Edwards put it, "inability," Edwards was distinguishing between "*moral* inability" and "*natural* inability." Unregenerate men possessed *natural* ability. God did not physically restrain their volition; but God had so constituted things that Adam's disobedience brought the entire human family under a condition of *moral* inability (Edwards 1879, 1:46-49, 281-88).

Fiering claimed that when Edwards wrote *Religious Affections* he had not become fully acquainted with the benevolist school. Sometime after 1746 he read Hutcheson's *Inquiry*. He had however been exposed to Shaftesbury's and Hutcheson's ideas via Chambers's *Cyclopedia* from which the longest quotation in *Religious Affections* was drawn. Fiering noted that Chambers had relied heavily upon Shaftesbury and Hutcheson in the volume on "Taste" from which Edwards had quoted.

> But despite this ... preliminary acquaintance with the benevolist school, Edwards could only have been amazed and dismayed when he first read Hutcheson's *Inquiry* and discovered in it arguments for a natural and universal moral

> sense that paralleled almost exactly what Edwards had been claiming exclusively for spiritual sense (Fiering 1981a, 129).

Edwards, Fiering noted, "began with spiritual relationships and descended to the material world," whereas Hutcheson "argued from material reality." Furthermore, Edwards insisted that the "so-called moral sense" of the benevolist school" was "solely an intellectual capacity and not psychologically related to affect" (1981a, 118).

Following Hutcheson, Joseph Butler (1692-1752) and David Hume (1711-1776) were to carry forward the benevolist theories with further modifications. T. A. Roberts stated that Butler refined Hutcheson's ideas giving a more detailed analysis of "compassion" and practically identifying self-love with benevolence. Hume's approach, according to Roberts, was "much more comprehensive, wide-ranging, and philosophically more fruitful" than Hutcheson's or Butler's (Avey [1954] 1961, 153; Roberts 1973, 76). Roberts pointed out that Hume "notoriously leaves God out of the picture," being satisfied to analyze benevolence in terms of "the natural virtues which belong to the essential nature of man."

Roberts further noted that Hume believed man was capable only of a "limited benevolence." Since that hypothesis was "based on observation" and only empirically true, Roberts reasoned, it was thus only "contingently true"--the future might invalidate the thesis (1973, 112). Roberts's analysis of the weakness of Hume's position was particularly significant, because Edwards's observations had already invalidated Hume's thesis. Edwards made some empirical observations during the revival at Northampton and recorded those observations in his *Narrative of the Surprising Work of God*--thereby documenting case histories of true benevolence in which self-interest was radically excised by the Spirit of God.

> Some express themselves, that they see the glory of God would *shine bright* in their own condemnation; and they are ready to think that if they are damned, they could take part with God against themselves, and would glorify his justice therein (Edwards 1879, 1:353).

What was for Hume, the object of horror, constituted, for Edwards, the foundation of benevolence and beauty.

> A truly virtuous mind, being as it were under the sovereign dominion of *love to God*, above all things, seeks the *glory of God*, and makes *this* his supreme, governing, and ultimate end. . . . And so far as a virtuous mind exercises true *benevolence* to created beings, it chiefly seeks the good of the creature; consisting in its *knowledge* or view of God's glory and beauty, its *union* with God, conformity and love to him, and joy in him (Edwards 1879, 1:127).

One final observation should be made in regard to David Hume. Roberts noted that the concept of the "lively simple idea" produced by a sensory or emotional impression was basic to Hume's philosophy (1973, 75-98).

Because of the difficulty in countering the naturalism of the benevolist school with its subtle pietistic underpinnings, Edwards's *True Virtue*, some have charged, suffered the intrusion of naturalistic ethics. "William Ames could fairly easily distinguish a Christian ethics from Aristotle's; Edwards faced the much harder task of distinguishing Christian ethics from Hutcheson's" (Fiering 1981a, 148-49).

> By the middle of the eighteenth century . . . nearly all the meaty psychological insight and schematizations of the churches, Protestant and Catholic, had been picked clean by the secular moral philosophers, leaving the clergy simply dry bones (Fiering 1981b, 194).

The new moral philosophy had absorbed Puritan pietistic principles and ideas, with their Augustinian roots, and had transmuted them into secular form. This made Edwards's task exceedingly difficult and may have accounted for "the relative intellectual poverty" of Edwards's *Original Sin* which "he was composing simultaneously with *True Virtue*."

> After so many concessions to natural human virtue, Original Sin as a *psychological* concept was approaching the vanishing point (Fiering 1981a, 148).

Norman Fiering cited two distinct phases of intense philosophical interest in Edwards's life.

> The first began in his earliest college days, extended through his tutorship at Yale, and lasted until he assumed pastoral duties in Northampton in 1727. The second phase began about 1746 and lasted until his death in 1758. The 20 years between 1727 and 1746 were in large part absorbed in working out the questions for the religious life posed by the Great Awakening, as well as by pastoral problems and responsibilities (1981a, Note, 106).

Whatever impact the benevolist school may have had upon Edwards prior to his reading Francis Hutcheson's *Inquiry*, the internal evidence of his writings suggested a thorough acquaintance with the new moral philosophy prior to 1746. There can be no doubt that Edwards's father, a 1694 Harvard graduate, had had a major introduction to the "new learning." Henry More's *Enchiridion Ethicum* (1667) had been adopted as the principal text for moral philosophy at Harvard in the 1680s. More's book, coupled with the arrival of Charles Morton, and the *de facto* leadership of John Leverett and William Brattle "extracted Harvard from the Scholastic pattern of ethics" (Fiering 1981b, 64, 207-94; Murray 1987, 5; Miller [1953] 1983, 237-38). An analysis of the "new learning" at Harvard lies beyond the scope of this book, and yet, the impact of Harvard upon the leadership of Puritan New England is beyond dispute--not even the Edwards's household was unaffected.

CHAPTER III

BENEVOLENCE AND THE BEATIFIC

Objectivism in Edwards

A contextual study of Edwards cannot disregard the striking similarity between Edwards's ethical system and that of Augustine and Malebranche both of whom contributed significantly (though separated by centuries) to the rise of the new moral philosophy. Augustine, while establishing an important role for the emotions, objectively grounded them in the doctrine of the Sovereign God. Linking self-love with "the cosmic love of God," Augustine affirmed "God's ontological position as the source of all good and beatitude" (O'Donovan 1980, 40). Augustine had regarded the Holy Spirit as the "self-love" of Deity or the mutual love that co-existed between the Father and the Son (O'Donovan 1980, 128, 134-35).

Nicolas Malebranche, though a disciple of Descartes, grounded his moral philosophy in the objective reality of God, who made his own "Glory" the "Principal End" for all his actions including the "Preservation of His Creatures." The only proper frame of reference for benevolence in Malebranche's system was the "Goodness" and "Subsistence" of God (Malebranche 1700, 138, 74, 147). Though the Third Earl of Shaftesbury regarded Malebranche as one of the three greatest philosophers of all time, Malebranche would sink into obscurity, by comparison with other moral philosophers of his day, being out of step with the rising relativism (Shaftesbury 1963, vol. 1, p. ix).

Jonathan Edwards would re-introduce theological objectivism into the realm of moral philosophy. It was noted in chapter 1 that Edwards's conversion was beatifically centered in the doctrine of divine sovereignty as his mind and heart came to a deep settledness and serenity concerning God's sovereign election, whereas the doctrine had previously been viewed with horror by Edwards (Edwards 1879, vol. 1, pp. liv-lv). For Edwards, that settled disposition of mind which the benevolist philosophers had described as "'the universal calm affection of good will towards all'" (Roberts 1973, 13), and which Edwards had observed in the youthful Sarah Pierrepont (Murray 1987, 92), was rooted in the Sovereign God. There was no ambivalence or unsettledness in the character or disposition of Deity. God's foreknowledge provided a certainty, indeed an infallibility, to benevolence as an ongoing ethical reality in the elect.

> To suppose the future volitions of moral agents not to be necessary events; or which is the same thing, events which it is not impossible but that they may not come to pass; and yet to suppose that God certainly foreknows them, and knows all things; is to suppose God's knowledge to be inconsistent with itself (Edwards 1879, 1:36).

> God, in the act of justification, which is passed on a sinner's first believing, has respect to perseverance, as being virtually contained in that first act of faith; and it is looked upon, and taken by him that justifies, as being as it were a property in that faith. God has respect to the believer's continuance in faith, and he is justified by that, as though it already were, because by divine establishment it shall follow; and it being by divine constitution connected with that first faith, as much as if it were a property in it, it is then considered as such, and so justification is not suspended; but were it not for this, it would be needful that it should be suspended, till the sinner had actually persevered in faith (Edwards 1879, 1:641).

Edwards's doctrine of divine foreknowledge was not simply a philosophical concession to George Berkeley (Fiering 1981a, 41-45); nor should Miller's assertion, that Edwards projected "the Lockean psychology into the Godhead," obscure the fact that Edwards's postulations of the psychological dimensions of Deity were solidly rooted in Scripture (Miller [1949] 1973, 298; Rom 8:28-30).

The student of Scripture will readily observe that, not only does Edwards's description of divine sovereignty in *Freedom of the Will* hang together by sheer force of logic, but it is also quite biblical.

> It is the glory and greatness of the Divine Sovereign, that his Will is determined by his own infinite, all-sufficient wisdom in every thing; and is in nothing at all directed either by inferior wisdom, or by no wisdom; whereby it would become senseless arbitrariness, determining and acting without reason, design or end (Edwards 1879, 1:71.)

> It derogates no more from the goodness of God to suppose the exercise of the benevolence of his nature to be determined by wisdom, than to suppose it determined by chance, and that his favors are bestowed altogether at random, his Will being determined by nothing but perfect accident, without any end or design whatsoever (Edwards 1879, 1:74).

For Edwards, there could be no virtue in any being who was arbitrary, undecided, or indifferent.

> So far is it from being agreeable to common sense, that such liberty as consists in indifference is requisite to Praise or Blame, that, on the contrary, the dictate of every man's natural sense through the world is, that the further he is from being indifferent in his acting good or evil, and the more he does either with full and strong inclination, the more he is esteemed or abhorred, commended or condemned (1879, 1:65).

It was axiomatic for Edwards that the will always acted according to "*the greatest apparent good*" (1979, 1:6). That "greatest apparent good" represented a "motive" which actually determined the disposition of the will. Thus the mind was never in a state of equilibrium but always determined and disposed by that motive.

> Every act of the Will whatsoever is excited by some motive: which is manifest, because, if the mind in willing after the manner it does, is excited by no motive or inducement, then it has no end which it proposes to itself, or pursues in so doing; it aims at nothing and seeks nothing (Edwards 1879, 1:26-27).

Edwards wrote his *Dissertation Concerning the End for Which God Created the World* to establish according to the "dictates of reason" and "divine revelation" that one thing in which God's "motive," or "end," consisted. The first five "dictates of reason" which Edwards set forth were as follows:

> 1. That no notion of God's last end in the creation of the world, is agreeable to reason, which would truly imply an indigence, insufficiency, and mutability in God: or any dependence of the Creator on the creature, for any part of his perfection or happiness. . . .
>
> 2. Whatsoever is good and valuable *in itself*, is worthy that God should value it with an *ultimate* respect. . . .
>
> 3. Whatsoever that be which is *in itself* most valuable, and what was so originally, prior to the creation of the world, and which is *attainable* by the creation, if there be any thing which was superior in value to all others, *that* must be worthy to be God's *last* end in the creation and also worthy to be his *highest* end. . . .
>
> 4. That if God *himself* be, in *any respect*, properly *capable* of being his own end in the creation of the world, then it is reasonable to suppose that he had respect to *himself*, as his last and highest end, in this work; because he is *worthy* in himself to be so, being infinitely the greatest and best of beings. . . . If God has respect to things according to their nature and proportions, he must necessarily have the greatest respect to himself (1879, 1:97-98)

In regard to the fourth "dictate" Edwards went on to say that

> the moral rectitude of the disposition, inclination, or affection of God CHIEFLY consists in a regard to HIMSELF, infinitely above his regard to all other beings; or, in other words, his holiness consists in this. . . .
>
> The *degree of regard* should always be in a *proportion compounded* of the *proportion* of *existence*, and *proportion* of *excellence* (1879, 1:98).

Continuing on, Edwards stated,

> 5. Whatsoever is good, amiable, and valuable *in itself*, *absolutely* and *originally*, (which facts and events show that

> God aimed at in the creation of the world,) must be supposed to be regarded or aimed at by God *ultimately*. . . .
> 6. Whatsoever thing is *actually* the *effect* of the creation of the world, which is simply and absolutely valuable in itself, that thing is an ultimate end of God's creating the world (1879, 1:99).

Proceeding from the above "dictates," Edwards went on to unfold the logic, as well as the scriptural basis, of God's making his own glory the highest end of everything he does. This doctrine would become the foundation of the *Nature of True Virtue* as well.

> It is evident, that the *divine* virtue, or the virtue of the divine mind, must consist primarily in *love to himself*, or in the mutual love and friendship which subsists eternally and necessarily between the several persons in the Godhead, or in that infinitely strong propensity there is in these divine persons one to another. . . . It will also follow, from the forgoing things that God's goodness and love to created beings, is derived from and subordinate to his love to himself (Edwards 1879, 1:126-27).

Thus the "wonderful alteration" in Edwards's mind whereby "an end was put to all those cavils and objections" against the doctrine of God's sovereignty, and whereby he came to a "*delightful* conviction" of divine sovereignty on the basis of 1 Tim 1:17, became the foundational experience for an ethical system based on the same beatific formula. As Augustine and Malebranche had affirmed before him, so Edwards would echo the theological refrain in praise of the God whose highest virtue, the foundation of all benevolence, was his own motive of *self-love*.

Ethics and Aesthetics

Edwards's doctrine of divine self-love was trinitarian in nature and was inextricably woven together with his aesthetic understanding of the faith. For Edwards, virtue was "consent to being" and, as there could be no consent for one person standing alone, the Trinity was an "ontological necessity" (Delattre 1968, 18; Gerstner 1987, 32). Accordingly, the Father's self-love made the begetting of the Son a necessity, and infinite mutual love between the Father and the Son logically presupposed the Holy Spirit who constituted the love of the

Father and the Son in action, "infinitely pure and perfect" (Gerstner 1987, 32-34). Fiering wrote,

> His entire moral theology is logically deducible from his theory of the Trinity alone, although unquestionably it worked the other way, too, and some of Edwards's insights into moral psychology contributed to his understanding of the Trinity (1981a, 82).

It was noted in the previous chapter that Shaftesbury had equated ethics with aesthetics thereby linking the "Good" with the "Beautiful" (Shaftesbury 1963, vol. 1, xxx). Although the beauty-virtue relationship was an ancient idea, Francis Hutcheson expounded it more than any previous philosopher (Fiering 1981a, 117). Edwards, like Hutcheson, discovered in aesthetics "an essential key to understanding and describing moral perceptions and moral conduct" (Fiering 1981a, 108); however, Edwards's concept of beauty, born of beatific vision and rooted in divine revelation, was of an infinitely higher order than that of the Shaftesbury-Hutcheson school, as "being" goes before "beauty," and "grace" exceeds "nature." In the *Nature of True Virtue* Edwards distinguished different levels of beauty.

> There is a beauty of understanding and speculation; there is something in the ideas and conceptions of great philosophers and statesmen, that may be called beautiful; which is a different thing from what is most commonly meant by virtue.
>
> But virtue is the beauty of those qualities or acts of the mind, that are of a *moral* nature, *i.e.* such as are attended with desert or worthiness of *praise* or *blame*. Things of this sort, it is generally agreed, so far as I know, do not belong merely to speculation; but to the *disposition* and *will*, or (to use a word, I suppose commonly well understood) to the *heart*. . . . So that when it is inquired, what is the nature of true *virtue*? this is the same as to inquire, what that is, which renders any habit, disposition, or exercise of the heart truly *beautiful*? (1879, 1:122)

After pointing out the distinction between a beauty of philosophical speculation and that beauty which was virtuous, having to do with the disposition of the heart, Edwards further differentiated between "*particular* beauty" and "*general* beauty"--the former being regarded within a limited context, the latter "viewed most perfectly, comprehensively, and universally, with regard to all its tendencies, and its connexions with every thing to which it stands related" (1879, 1:122). Thus *true* virtue was "beautiful by a *general* beauty or beautiful in a comprehensive view"--or, in more metaphysical terms, "True virtue most essentially consists in BENEVOLENCE TO BEING IN GENERAL."

> Perhaps, to speak more accurately, it is that consent, propensity, and union of heart to being in general, which is immediately exercised in a general good will (Edwards 1879, 1:122).

A key to understanding Edwards's *Dissertation Concerning the Nature of True Virtue* is the enigmatic metaphysical expression "being in general." *True Virtue* was originally published in 1765 through the efforts of Samuel Hopkins conjointly with *A Dissertation Concerning the End for Which God Created the World* under the title *Two Dissertations* (Murray 1987, 449). Hopkins knew well that the two dissertations properly belonged together. Edwards in *The End for Which God Created the World* had defined the term "being in general" as "the system . . . comprehending the *sum total* of universal existence, both Creator and creature" (1879, 1:98). Consequently, when Edwards defined true virtue as "consent" to, or "union of heart" with, "being in general," he was excluding any private or limited ethical expressions which did not properly regard the whole of reality--created and uncreated beings--with the exception, of course, of inanimate things which lacked perception and will (1879, 1:123).

Affirming a generally accepted notion that the essence of virtue was love (1879, 1:122-23), Edwards went on to distinguish between two kinds of love--"love of benevolence and love of complacence." Love of benevolence was

> that affection, or propensity of the heart to any being, which causes it to incline to its well-being, or disposes it to desire or take pleasure in its happiness (1879, 1:123).

"Love of *benevolence*" was not contingent upon, or necessarily related to, any beauty in the object of affection. "Love of *complacence*" presupposed beauty in the object of affection. Since "love of *complacence*" made beauty the foundation of love, equating virtue with the love of virtue, Edwards recognized the circular nature of such a proposition and rejected "complacence," and any benevolence based on beauty, as in any way being foundational for virtue. He insisted, instead, that "the *first* object of a virtuous benevolence" was "*being* simply considered." Therefore the object possessing the "greatest share of existence" was properly entitled to the "*greatest* share of the propensity and benevolent affections of the heart." "Pure benevolence," consequently, was "in its *first* exercise" the matter of "being's uniting consent, or propensity to being" (1879, 1:123).

"The *second* object of a virtuous propensity of heart," according to Edwards was "*benevolent being*"--which was to say that the benevolent disposition of intelligent beings toward other beings ought to have been commensurate with the degree of benevolence which those other beings held toward "being in general." Thus, it was plain that while Edwards's ethics were cast in an aesthetic frame, the system had its foundation in ontology. Beauty was defined according to "being." Ontology was more fundamental than aesthetics.

It was only proper, on the first hand, that one would be virtuously disposed toward a being in proportion to the measure of his share of being and, secondly, virtuously disposed toward other beings in proportion to their regard for the same principle. The one who had the greatest share of being was properly entitled to the greatest share of benevolence; and those who had the greatest respect for being, on the widest possible scale, ought be the objects of greatest love. They were beautiful in proportion to their regard for "being in general" and were the objects of the love of complacence only on that basis. Conversely, a person was despicable in proportion to the degree to which he asserted his own private interest above the wider interests of the entire general existence of which he held but a small share (Edwards 1879, 1:123).

On this basis, it was but a simple step in logic for Edwards to affirm that in regard both to the first objective ground of love, as well as to the second, true virtue "must chiefly consist in LOVE TO GOD; the Being of beings, infinitely the greatest and best."

> God has infinitely the greatest share of existence. So that all other being, even the whole universe, is as nothing in comparison of the Divine Being (Edwards 1879, 1:125).

Furthermore,

> as God is infinitely the greatest Being, so he is allowed to be infinitely the most beautiful and excellent: and all the beauty to be found throughout the whole creation, is but the reflection of the diffused beams of that Being who hath an infinite fullness of brightness and glory (Edwards 1879, 1:125).

Edwards went on to say, what has previously been noted, that God's chief virtue consisted "primarily in *love to himself*, or in the mutual love and friendship which subsists eternally and necessarily between the several persons of the Godhead." Therefore Edwards's definition of true virtue as "consent" to "being in general" was consistent with the chief virtue of God, viz., his infinite consent to his own being as "the head of the universal system of existence." It followed that "a disposition to love God Supremely" was tantamount to "a benevolent propensity of heart to being in general" (Edwards 1879, 1:125-27).

It was a simple matter then for Edwards to define *primary* beauty as "*cordial* consent" to, or "union" with, "being in general," in order to convey, in the idiom of moral philosophy, the biblical concepts of "GRACE" and "HOLINESS" (1879, 1:127-28).

> Edwards's goal was to transfer the idea of holiness from its isolation in the temples of religion and make of it a philosophically credible notion in the forums of enlightenment. The substance of holiness was not changed, but its new name, in conformity to the age, would be "true virtue" (Fiering 1981a, 106).

Hutcheson had defined beauty as "uniformity in the midst of variety." This for Edwards was an inferior kind of beauty which he regarded as "secondary beauty." God had so constituted the world that this secondary beauty--harmony of sounds, proportion, agreement of colors, and symmetry--served as an external image or analogy of the true virtue consisting of cordial consent to being in general (Edwards 1879, 1:127-28). But primary beauty was distinct from secondary beauty.

> Who will affirm, that a disposition to approve of the harmony of good music, or the beauty of a square, or equilateral triangle, is the same with true holiness, or a truly virtuous disposition of mind (Edward 1879, 1:129).

Edwards went on to demonstrate that immaterial things, as well, such as a natural disposition toward "justice," "duties toward relatives," "gratitude," and even "conscience" itself were but *secondary* expressions of beauty, concerns of proportion and uniformity neither involving "cordial consent" to being in general, nor holiness in the heart (1879, 1:128-29, 133). Such things were no more truly virtuous than "the taste of honey" or "the smell of a rose" (Edwards 1879, 1:130).

It may be observed from the foregoing analysis of *Nature of True Virtue*, that, for Edwards, in the matter of ethics, ontology held a higher priority than aesthetics--*existence* came before *excellence*, *being* before *beauty*. For Shaftesbury and Hutcheson the reverse was true (Fiering 1981a, 108).

> The corrective against aestheticism in Edwards' deployment of beauty as the primary model of order in the moral world as well as the natural world lies in his objectivist definition of beauty and in his systematic insistence that virtue and holiness and spiritual beauty are founded not in consent to beauty but in consent to being (Delattre 1968, 25).

Fiering pointed out that the "similarity between the perception of 'external beauty' and the perception of true virtue and holiness," as Edwards postulated it, lay in "the immediacy by which the knowledge is gained" as opposed to "'a train of reasoning'." There was no *substantive* resemblance involved (1981a, 120). Roland Delattre in *Beauty and Sensibility in the Thought of Jonathan Edwards* stated,

> In settling upon beauty as the most distinguishing perfection or attribute of God he chose a concept that enabled him to conceive of God in objective, structural, and ontological terms and at the same time to make it philosophically (and not merely dogmatically) clear that (and why) God can be fully known only if He is the direct object of enjoyment--that man's knowledge of God is in part a function of his enjoyment of Him. With his objectivist concept of beauty, Edwards can insist upon the objectivity of God while also affirming that God cannot be adequately known without being enjoyed. For beauty is objective with respect to the self, and yet it is available only in and through the enjoyment of it (1968, 23-24).

Delattre might have more accurately represented Edwards's thought, if instead of suggesting Edwards had settled upon beauty as "the most distinguishing perfection or attribute of God," he had merely suggested that Edwards chose beauty as an *idiom of divine holiness* (Fiering 1981a, 80-81).

> As the beauty of the divine nature primarily consists in God's holiness, so does the beauty of all divine things (Edwards 1879, 1:279).
>
> Holiness is in a peculiar manner the beauty of the divine nature. Hence we often read of the *beauty of holiness* [Psal. xxix.2. Psal. xcvi.9. and cx.3.] (Edwards 1879, 1:279).

Expressing holiness in terms of beauty, Edwards knew, was a scriptural notion (Edwards 1879, 1:279). The above attempt to qualify, or clarify, Delattre's comments, therefore, must not obscure Delattre's essential point that the use of the aesthetic by Edwards enabled him to affirm "the objectivity of God while also affirming that God cannot be known without being enjoyed." To put it another way, Edwards could not have spoken of ethics in aesthetic idiom without, at the same time, addressing the related issues of disinterested benevolence versus self-love, and holiness versus happiness. The sum of the matter had been succinctly expressed a century earlier in the Westminster Shorter Catechism: "Man's chief end is to glorify God, and to enjoy him for ever" (Committee n.d., Q. 1). Edwards would spell it out.

Disinterested Benevolence versus Self-Love

Delattre stated that "disinterestedness" for Edwards did not mean "an absence of interest or of subjectivity but rather a passionate interest in conforming the subjective order of pleasure to the objective order of beauty" (1968, 23). Before an examination of Edwards's doctrine of "disinterestedness," it is important to mention that the matter of motive had long been an issue of concern among Puritans, and there was no unanimity on the question. Joseph Alleine in the seventeenth century had insisted on the highest of motives in coming to Christ in *An Alarm to the Unconverted.*

> But the sound convert desires holiness for holiness' sake; and not merely for heaven's sake. He would not be satisfied with so much as might save him from hell, but desires the highest degree (Alleine 1959, 27).

John Bunyan, on the other hand, in his magnificent sermon on John 6:37 entitled *Come and Welcome to Jesus Christ*, pictured the sinner's first objection to coming to Christ in the following way: "I fear my ends are not right. . . . My end is that I might have life and be saved by Jesus Christ." To this objection Bunyan responded,

> To come to Christ *for life, and to be saved*: though at present thou hast *no* other end, is a lawful, and good coming to Jesus Christ. . . . Christ propoundeth life as the only argument to prevail with sinners in coming to him, and so blameth them because they come not to him for life (Bunyan 1979, 260).

Bunyan stated the sinner's second objection as follows:

> When, I say, I only seek myself, I mean, I do not find that I do design God's glory in mine own salvation by Christ, and that makes me fear, I do not come aright (1979, 262).

To this second objection Bunyan responded,

> Where doth Christ Jesus requireth such a Qualification, of those that are coming to him for life? Come thou for life, and trouble not thy head with such objections against thy self, and let God and Christ alone to glorify themselves in the salvation of such a worm as thou art. . . . He hast no need of thy designs, though thou hast need of his. . . . The Jayler was only for knowing at first, what he should do to be saved: But *Paul* did not so much as once ask him, what is your end in this question; do you design the Glory of God in the salvation of your soul? (1979, 263-64).

Thus, the motive question was not original with Edwards but was a deeply rooted Puritan issue. As noted in the previous chapter, it was also a significant issue in the new moral philosophy. Locke had caricatured Christians as predicating their ethical decisions on the basis of future rewards and punishments (Locke 1952, 105). The Third Earl of Shaftesbury, had insisted that there was no virtue in a benevolence toward God which was based on future rewards and punishments (Shaftesbury 1963, vol. 1, p. xxx). Against this background Edwards was to set forth his own statement on the motive matter.

In part 3, section 2, of the *Religious Affections*, Edwards gave what was to be his strongest statement of the doctrine of disinterested benevolence.

> *The first objective ground of gracious affections, is the transcendently excellent and amiable nature of divine things, as they are in themselves; and not any conceived relation they bear to self, or self-interest* (1879, 1:274).

> Now the divine *excellency* of God, and of Jesus Christ, the word of God, his works, ways, & c. [etc.] is the primary reason why a true saint loves these things; and not any supposed *interest* he has in them, or any conceived benefit that he has received or shall receive from them (1879, 1:275).

Edwards then proceeded to answer the objections of those who insisted that all love was founded on *self-love*.

> They argue, that whoever loves God, and so desires his glory, or the enjoyment of him, desires these things as his own happiness. . . . But then they ought to consider a little further, and inquire how the man *came to place* his *happiness* in God's being glorified. . . . There is no doubt, but that after God's glory, and beholding his perfections are become *agreeable* to him, he will desire them, as he does his own happiness. . . . Must not a man first *love* God, or have his heart united to him, before he will esteem God's good his own, and before he will desire the glorifying and enjoying of God, as his own happiness (1879, 1.275).

Edwards argued that to say a man after loving God discovers a happiness so personally satisfying that he wants to go on loving God is not to say that the original love of God was based on self-love.

> If *after* a man loves God, it will be a *consequence* and *fruit of this,* that even love to his own happiness will cause him to desire the glorifying and enjoying of God; it will not thence follow, that this very exercise of self-love went *before* his love to God, and that his love to God was a *consequence and fruit of that*. Something else, entirely distinct from self-love, might be the cause of this, *viz.* a change made in the views of his

> mind, and relish of his heart; whereby he apprehends a beauty, glory, and supreme good, in God's nature, as it is in itself (1879, 1:275).

Edwards insisted that I John 4:19: "We love because he first loved us" (NIV), was not to be understood as setting forth an egoistic motive for love, but on the contrary--"he loved us, while we had no love to him" (1879, 1:277).

> They whose affection to God is founded first on his *profitableness* to them, begin at the wrong end (Edwards 1879, 1:275).

It was evident from Edwards's doctrine of disinterested benevolence that self-love did have a legitimate role to play in religious experience, but it was not a foundational role. Just as Edwards had acknowledged a legitimate place for secondary beauty as a subordinate and supportive concept to primary beauty, so self-love had its function in subordination to, and support of, the saints' love for God. "Disinterest" for Edwards was not "uninterest" as it had been for Shaftesbury (Delattre 1968, 23; Shaftesbury 1963, vol. 1, p. xxx; Dwight 1863, 487-96).

> Indeed the saints rejoice in their interest in God, and that Christ is theirs; and so they have great reason: but this is not the first spring of their joy. They first rejoice in God as glorious and excellent in himself, and then secondarily rejoice in it, that so glorious a God is theirs. . . . But that which is the true *saint's superstructure* is the *hypocrite's foundation* (Edwards 1879, 1:277).

It was noted earlier that both Malebranche and Edwards regarded self-love as a God-given instinct for the preservation of mankind but that consequent to the Fall, with the loss of the principle of holiness, the inferior principles of self-love became "masters of the heart"--and therein was the essence of sin (Edwards 1879, 1:217-18; Malebranche 1700, 147). Self-love in proper proportion and in subordination to the spirit of holiness was not evil and indeed partook of the virtuous beauty of holiness, but standing alone it could not be considered truly virtuous. "Pure benevolence" could indeed mix its influence with the natural principles of self-love so that natural compassion could become "virtuous compassion."

> So there is a virtuous *gratitude*; or a gratitude that arises not only from self-love, but from a superior principle of disinterested general benevolence. . . . And as, when *natural affections* have their operations *mixed* with the influence of virtuous benevolence, and are *directed* and *determined* thereby, they may be called *virtuous*; so there may be a *virtuous* love of parents to children, and between other near relatives; a *virtuous* love of our town, or country, or nation. Yea, and a *virtuous* love between the sexes, as there may be the influence of virtue *mingled* with instinct (Edwards 1879, 1:139).

There was one sense in which Edwards used the term self-love that was morally neutral. Edwards stated that self-love could be taken to mean a person's "loving whatsoever is pleasing to him" which could be reduced to "loving what he loves"--"which is the same thing as a man's having a faculty of will" (1879, 1:130).

> If he is capable of having inclination, will and choice, then what he inclines to, and chooses, is grateful to him, whatever that be; whether it be his own private good, the good of his neighbors, or the glory of God. And so far as it is grateful or pleasing to him, so far is it a part of his pleasure, good, or happiness (1879, 1:130).

Edwards argued that if that were all that were meant by self-love, then to ask whether all love arose from self-love was as meaningless as to ask whether fixing our love on particular objects was due to our capacity to love some things (1879, 1:130).

This morally neutral concept of self-love which Edwards reduced to the simple matter of a person's faculty of will was roughly equivalent to Gordon Clark's concept of "psychological hedonism" which, he said, had nothing to do with ethics since it described "what is," not "what ought to be" ([1952] 1960, 163-66). Edwards was careful, however, to disassociate any hedonistic traces as foundational principles in the Christian motive.

> That a man in general loves, and is pleased with happiness, or has a capacity of enjoying happiness, cannot be the reason why such and such things become his happiness. . . .
>
> For here the effect is made the cause of that of which it is the effect: our happiness, consisting in the happiness of the person beloved, is made the cause of our love to that person. Whereas the truth plainly is, that our love to that person is the cause of our delighting or being happy in his happiness. . . . Men who have benevolence to others have pleasure when they see others' happiness, because seeing their happiness gratifies some inclination that was in their hearts before (1879, 1:130).

Proceeding from the definition of self-love as the faculty of will, Edwards demonstrated, somewhat "hedonistically," the logic of a disposition toward the happiness of "being in general."

> There is no other temper but this, whereby a man can agree with himself, or be without self-inconsistency, *i.e.* without having some inclinations and relishes repugnant to others; and for these reasons. Every being that has understanding and will necessarily loves happiness. For, to suppose any being not to love happiness, would be to suppose he did not love what was agreeable to him; which is a contradiction: or at least would imply, that nothing was agreeable or eligible to him, which is the same as to say that he has no such thing as choice, or any faculty of will. So that every being who has a faculty of will, must of necessity have an inclination to happiness. And therefore, if he be consistent with himself, and has not some inclinations repugnant to others, he must approve of those inclinations whereby beings desire the happiness of being in general, and must be against a disposition to the misery of being in general: because otherwise he would approve of opposition to his own happiness. For if a temper inclined to the misery of being in general prevailed universally, it is apparent, it would tend to universal misery. But he that loves a tendency to *universal* misery, in effect loves a tendency to his *own* misery. . . . But if men loved hatred to being in general, they would in effect love the hatred of *themselves* (1879, 1:141).

The above statement, while demonstrating the finely-knit logic of Edwards, also illustrated the difficulty in keeping the doctrine of disinterested benevolence free from the intrusions of self-love; for such logic can scarcely be anything less than an appeal to virtue on the basis of self-love, albeit defined as a faculty of the will. Edwards, like Augustine, certainly opened his system to "eudaemonism" by such a statement (O'Donovan 1980, 142). And yet, even though Edwards could appeal on the basis of self-interest, it was clearly in his mind a subordinate concept as has been noted. Fiering pointed out that William Ames had "allowed subordinate ends, such as self-interest, to be *part* of love to God and also to be part of one's quest for salvation," and that his opinion represented a long-standing tradition (Fiering 1981a, 156).

Fiering distinguished four forms of self-love in Edwards's writings. The *first* was "a universal psychological principle of seeking happiness defined as that which is agreeable to oneself, true of all creatures in heaven and hell and of God himself" (1981a, 159). This expression of self-love, tantamount to the faculty of will, has just been discussed. By this definition, good and evil were relative to the "good" as perceived by the one who chose, as illustrated in the cry of resolute despair by Milton's Lucifer: "Evil, be thou my good" (Milton [1949] 1961, 314); although Edwards would have questioned whether anyone, even Satan himself, could have delighted in his own misery without, of course, being divided against himself (Edwards 1879, 1:141; Matt 12:36).

The *second* form of self-love Fiering noted in Edwards's works was "the seeking of one's own exclusive good, which necessarily is at the cost of other people, called 'simple self-love' (and in common language, selfishness)" (1981a, 159). This was self-love in its most restricted sense, and, in Edwards's words, signified "a man's regard to his confined *private self*, or love to himself with respect to his *private interest*" (1879, 1:130). But there was a *third* form of self-love, Fiering noted, which was an extension of the *second* and to which Edwards referred as "'compounded self-love.'" Fiering described this as "an enlarged sense of one's own good, which may include others to a greater or lesser degree." He stated that it could be traced to "a process of reasoning" later described as "'enlightened self-interest'" or to "natural instincts that propel men into caring for others" (1981a, 159-60). It has already been noted that these *second* and *third* forms were those divinely-bestowed principles which had expanded to monstrous proportions via the Fall and could only be considered virtuous as they were subordinated to the Spirit of holiness in the soul of a regenerate person (Edwards 1879, 1:139, 217-18).

Fiering, in addition to these first three expressions, distinguished a *fourth* form of self-love in Edwards--

> a measured and proportional esteem for oneself in relation to the created universe of goods, whereby one loves oneself as a creature of God, which may be called limited self-regard (1981a, 160).

This "measured and proportional self-esteem" or "limited self-regard" was, in this writer's judgment, considerably more elusive than the first three forms cited by Fiering; though it must have been brought about by the infused grace of regeneration whereby a man's heart became inclined toward a love of God and the soul experienced divine happiness. Consequently the natural self-love (of Fiering's *second* and *third* forms), so destitute of virtue standing alone, became gloriously restored to its fitting proportion and position of beatitude in subordination to the superior principle of love to God.

On this basis of enjoyment of God, the idea that any believer could ever wish to be eternally damned for the glory of God involved a contradiction (Fiering 1981a, 160). Indeed Edwards had rejected such an idea as being far beyond the biblical requirement. Noting how some under the convictions of spiritual awakening at Northampton were impressed with their own unworthiness to the extent of being almost willing to be damned, Edwards stated "It must be owned that they had not clear and distinct ideas of damnation, nor does any word in the Bible require such self-denial as this" (Edwards 1879, 1:353; Fiering 1981a, 160).

For Edwards, self-love, properly defined, was "an irremovable and acceptable substratum" rather than the primary ethical incentive (Fiering 1981a, 152). Edwards in *Charity and Its Fruits* commented, "'In some respects wicked men do not love themselves enough--not so much as the godly do; for they do not love the way of their own welfare and happiness'" (Fiering 1981a, 171). Fiering, however, misstated the case for Edwards when he said,

> God's self-love is thus a model of proper self-love. Men, too, as part of the creation may properly love themselves provided that their love is *proportional* to that which is good in themselves. This is simply appropriate self-esteem (1981a, 154).

It is doubtful whether Edwards acknowledged anything amiable in man in his natural state apart from God's grace. Even in his regenerate state, Edwards examined his heart in the light of beatific vision and exclaimed,

> The very thought of any joy arising in me, on any consideration of my own amiableness, performances, or experiences, or any goodness of heart or life, is nauseous and detestable to me (1879, vol. 1, p. xc).

Edwards knew that even "the holy acts" and "gracious exercises of the godly" were "defective" (Edwards 1879, 1:644).

Holiness and Happiness

The happiness which the saint enjoyed was a delight in God's holiness. It was not so much a delight in the believer's progress in sanctification as a delight in God's grace and acceptance of the believer, who in spite of his unworthiness, was made a partaker of divine holiness.

> For the least sin against an infinite God, has an infinite hatefulness or deformity in it; but the highest degree of holiness in a creature has not an infinite loveliness in it: and therefore the loveliness of it is as nothing, in comparison of the deformity of the least sin. . . . and if a Being be infinitely lovely or worthy to be loved by us, then our obligations to love him are infinitely great: and therefore, whatever is contrary to this love, has in it infinite iniquity, deformity, and unworthiness (Edwards 1879, 1:298).

Edwards continued,

> But on the other hand, with respect to our holiness or love to God, there is not an infinite worthiness in that. The sin of the creature against God, is ill-deserving and hateful in proportion to the distance there is between God and the creature: the

greatness of the object, and the meanness and inferiority of the subject, aggravate it. But it is the reverse with regard to the worthiness of the respect of the creature to God; it is *worthless*, and not worthy, in proportion to the meanness of the subject. So much the greater the distance between God and the creature, so much the less is the creature's respect worthy of God's notice or regard. The great degree of superiority increases the obligation on the inferior to regard the superior; and so makes the want of regard more hateful (1879, 1:298).

Edwards relentlessly argued,

> It most demonstrably appears, that true grace is of that nature, that the more a person has of it, with remaining corruption, the less does his goodness and holiness appear, in proportion to his deformity; and not only to his past, but to his present deformity, in the sin that now appears in his heart and in the abominable defects of his highest and best affections, and brightest experiences (1879, 1:298).

Following these statements relative to principles of holiness, Edwards shared his own misgivings regarding some of those affected during the revival fires of the Great Awakening.

> The nature of many high religious affections, and great discoveries (as they are called) in many persons I have been acquainted with, is to hide the corruption of their hearts, and to make it seem to them as if all their sin was gone, and to leave them without complaints of any hateful evil left in them; (though it may be they cry out much of their past unworthiness;) a sure and certain sign that their discoveries are darkness and not light. It is darkness that hides men's pollution and deformity; but light let into the heart discovers it, searches it out in its secret corners, and makes it plainly to appear; especially that penetrating, all-searching light of God's holiness and glory (1879, 1:298-99).

Such was the effect of God's holiness upon the soul that

> the children of God never have such a *sensible* and *spiritual* conviction of their deformity, and so great, quick, and abasing sense of their present vileness and odiousness, as when they are highest in the exercise of true grace (Edwards 1879, 1:299).

Thus, for Edwards, self-esteem in the life of the believer would be inversely proportional to the experience of God's grace and holiness in the believer's heart, and it appears highly unlikely that Edwards could ever have represented God's self-love as a model of proper self-love in humans. Self-esteem, inversely proportional to the experience of God's grace and holiness, would have reduced such a notion to absurdity.

Holiness represented, for Edwards, God's essential *moral* attribute as distinct from his *natural* attributes of omniscience and omnipotence. He stated, "There is no other *true virtue* but *real holiness*" (1879, 1:279).

> The true beauty and loveliness of all intelligent beings primarily and most essentially consist in their moral excellency or holiness. . . . Strength and knowledge do not render any being lovely without holiness, but more hateful; though they render them more lovely when joined with holiness. Thus the elect angels are the more glorious for their strength and knowledge, because these natural perfections of theirs are sanctified by their moral perfection. But though the devils are very strong, and of great natural understanding, yet they are not the more lovely. They are more *terrible*, indeed, not more *amiable*; but on the contrary, the more hateful. The holiness of an intelligent creature, is the *beauty* of all his natural perfections. And so it is in God, according to our way of conceiving of the Divine Being: holiness is in a peculiar manner the beauty of the divine nature (Edwards 1879, 1:279).

And if holiness was God's essential moral attribute, as Edwards had so poignantly affirmed in the above passages from the *Religious Affections*, God would take special delight in the "emanation" or "communication" of that attribute of his being to other intelligent beings.

> As God delights in his own beauty, he must necessarily delight in the creature's holiness; which is a conformity to and participation of it, as truly as a brightness of a jewel held in the sun's beams is a participation or a derivation of the sun's brightness, though immensely less in degree (Edwards 1879, 1:101).

In the *End for Which God Created the World* Edwards would tell "wherein this holiness in the creature consists, viz. in love, which is the comprehension of all virtue; and primarily in love to God." God's supreme delight in his own glory moved him to communicate or diffuse his own "FULLNESS" to the creature. As God delighted in his own glory and excellence, so he took special pleasure in the diffusion or manifestation of the fullness of that glory and excellence among his creatures. The *knowledge* of himself, the virtue of his *holiness*, and the blessing of his *happiness* were among the aspects of God's communicated fullness which Edwards singled out (1879, 1:100-101). God's happiness which he communicated to the creatures was a happiness which he took in himself; the creatures' happiness consisted of their enjoyment of God's glory.

> This happiness consists in enjoying and rejoicing in himself; and so does also the creature's happiness. It is a participation of what is in God; and God is the objective ground of it. The happiness of the creature consists in rejoicing in God; by which also God is magnified and exalted (Edwards 1879, 1:101).

Thus, for Edwards, there was a direct connection between holiness and happiness. One could not have one without the other, even as the Westminster brethren had linked the two: "Man's chief and highest end is to glorify God, and fully to enjoy him forever" (Committee n.d., Lg. Cat., Q. 1). Edwards insisted that the pleasure God took in seeing the *happy state* of the recipients of his benevolent love could not be distinguished from the delight which he took in the complacent love within his own being.

> This delight which God has in his creature's happiness, cannot properly be said to be what God receives from the creature. For it is only the effect of his own work in and communications to the creature; in making it, and admitting it to a participation of his fullness. As the sun receives nothing from the jewel that receives its light, and shines only by a participation of its brightness (Edwards 1879, 1:102).

Thus it was apparent that God, in bringing about the creature's happiness, maintained his own sovereign glory. Public happiness was not God's highest end, nor was it to be the highest end of his creatures; but rather, God, in seeking his own happiness, ultimately established public happiness. Edwards's view of happiness, unlike the view of the secular moral philosophers, was inseparably linked to holiness. The very foundation of God's own happiness in Edwards's view, was God's own holiness.

> With respect also to the creature's *holiness*; God may have a proper delight and joy in imparting this to the creature, as gratifying hereby his inclination to communicate of his own excellent fullness. God may delight, with true and great pleasure, in beholding that beauty which is an image and communication of his own beauty, an expression and manifestation of his own loveliness. And this is so far from being an instance of his happiness not being in and from himself, that it is an evidence that he is happy in himself, or delights and takes pleasure in his own beauty. If he did not take pleasure in the *expression* of his own beauty, it would rather be an evidence that he does not *delight* in his own beauty; that he hath not his happiness and enjoyment in his own beauty and perfection (1879, 1:102).

Joseph Haroutunian was close to the mark when he called Edwards a "'theologian of the Great Commandment'" (Cherry [1966] 1974, 77). Clyde Holbrook stated that the key to understanding Edwards's ethics was his "theological objectivism" (Holbrook 1973, 1-9; Lesser 1981, 319). Holbrook described Edwards's moral philosophy as "an ethic of responsibility which moves more by attraction of the final good in being than by the stern call of duty" (Holbrook 1973, 185). The summation and analysis of Edwards's writings set forth in this chapter are consistent with these expressed conclusions of Haroutunian and Holbrook.

It was quite apparent that benevolence, in Edwards's system, was predicated upon the delight which God took in the greatness of his own Being which comprehended all existence and excellence. There could be no benevolence apart from cordial consent to the Being of beings through regeneration--the implantation of the principle of holiness. By contemplating the beauty of holiness in regeneration, a man came to discover his highest happiness in the glory of God. This was the dawning of beatific vision and the foundation of benevolence. Thus man could both "glorify God and . . . enjoy him forever" (Edwards 1879, 1:125; Committee n.d., Sh. Cat., Q. 1).

CHAPTER IV

CALVIN, THE COVENANT, AND THE BEATIFIC

Edwards and Dort's Five Points

Edwards's "theological objectivism," according to Clyde Holbrook, was Calvinistic in nature (Holbrook 1973, 4-5). Conrad Cherry wrote,

> For good or ill, Edwards was a Calvinist theologian; and, as a Calvinist theologian, he claimed the heritage of his New England forefathers ([1966] 1974, 3).

The impact of Calvinism upon New England, as well as upon the other American colonies, was well illustrated by a letter sent to John Wesley by George Whitefield at the height of the Great Awakening. Upon hearing that Wesley had accepted Arminian views, Whitefield urged him to remain in England and suggested Wesley's ministry would not be effective in America where the Awakening had been precipitated by Calvinistic preaching (Heimert and Miller 1967, xxvi).

Carl Bogue in *Jonathan Edwards and the Covenant of Grace* stated, "No issue is so fundamental to the understanding of Edwards the theologian as the Calvinist-Arminian controversy." The Puritan pastor-theologian of Northampton "saw Arminianism as the issue and the enemy in the New England of his day" (Bogue 1975, 77).

In 1737 Edwards wrote his personal documentary on the revival which had taken place at Northampton. It was entitled *A Faithful Narrative of the Surprising Work of God, in the Conversion of Many Hundred Souls, in Northampton, and the Neighboring Towns and Villages of New Hampshire, in New England; in a Letter to the Rev. Dr. Colman of Boston*. In his general introductory statement describing the circumstances which preceded the revival, Edwards referred to "the great *noise* . . . about *Arminianism*, which seemed to appear with a very *threatening* aspect upon the interest of religion here" and to "some things said *publicly* on that occasion, concerning *justification by faith alone*." Edwards's series of teachings "proved a word spoken in season . . . and was most evidently attended with a very remarkable blessing of heaven to the souls of the people in this town" (Edwards 1879, 1:347-48).

Perry Miller in his biography of Edwards minimized the seriousness of the Arminian threat in New England.

> In 1726 Cotton Mather boasted that there was not one Arminian in New England; yet here was Edwards in 1734 asserting, as though desperately rescuing the churches from imminent danger of this very heresy, that we are abominable creatures in the sight of God, that our righteousness is ten thousand times less than nothing, and that the majesty of God is more worthily exhibited if He delivers such vagabonds without any virtue on their part than if He should reward their righteousness (Miller [1949] 1973, 106-107).

Conrad Cherry, in an attempt to correct the misimpression left by Miller, mentioned that not only were there defections of some New England clergy to Arminianism in their embracing Episcopalianism, but that in the 1730s there were young men remaining within Congregationalist ranks who were imbibing Arminian notions. Edwards's cousin Israel Williams had strongly objected to Edwards's involvement in the investigation of a pastoral candidate suspected of espousing Arminian principles, and this conflict marked the beginning of a long-standing animosity of the Williams family toward Jonathan Edwards (Cherry [1966] 1974, 186-87; Murray 1987, 334-35, 373-83, 424-25; Edwards 1879, 1:485-531).

Years later, as Edwards was confronting the views of English Arminian John Taylor in *Freedom of the Will*, he stated the basis on which he so strongly opposed the Arminian scheme.

> The doctrine of a self-determining will . . . teaches a kind of absolute independence on all those things, that are of chief importance in this affair; our righteousness depending originally on our own acts as self-determined. Thus our own holiness is from ourselves, as its determining cause, and its original and highest source. And as for imputed righteousness, that should have any merit at all in it, to be sure, there can be no such thing. For self-determination is necessary to praise and merit. But what is imputed from another is not from our self-determination or action. And truly, in this scheme, man is not dependent on God; but God is rather dependent on man . . .
>
> The nature of true faith implies a disposition, to give all the glory of our salvation to God and Christ. But this notion is inconsistent with it, for it in effect gives the glory wholly to man. For that is the very doctrine that is taught, that the merit and praise is his, whose is the original and effectual determination of the praiseworthy deed (Bogue 1975, 232).

Thus Edwards's rejection of the Arminian system was on the basis of his commitment to the glory of God. In Edwards's judgment, Arminianism glorified man rather than God. The title of Edwards's famous Public Lecture in Boston, July 8, 1731, shortly after he assumed full pastoral responsibilities at Northampton, was itself indicative of Edwards's theological standard: *God Glorified in Man's Dependence* (Murray 1987, 107-108). The system of Christian doctrine adopted at the Synod of Dort (Steele and Thomas 1963), which had come to be known as Calvinism, did just that--it glorified God in man's dependence. Those doctrines of total depravity, unconditional election, limited atonement, irresistible grace, and the perseverance of the saints thrust man totally upon the grace of God for salvation resulting in God's glory.

> All five of Dort's points were claimed by Edwards as necessary defenses of God's power and glory in the salvation of man and as necessary means of preventing the ascription of power and glory to man instead (Cherry [1966] 1974, 189).

In his defense of the doctrine of *total depravity* against the Arminian challenge, Edwards argued,

> Now this doctrine supposes *no other necessity* of sinning, than a moral necessity; which, as has been shown, does not at all excuse sin; and *no other inability* to obey any command, or perform any duty, even the most spiritual and exalted, but a moral inability, which . . . does not excuse persons in the non-performance of any good thing, or make them not to be the proper objects of commands, counsels and invitations (1879, 1:87).

Edwards could affirm total depravity and, with equal force, affirm the necessity of obedience to the commands of God because

> every such act of obedience, wherein it is inward, and the act of the soul, is only a new effective act of reception of Christ, and adherence to the glorious Savior (Edwards 1879, 1:642).

In this regard Edwards was like Augustine. In his *Confessions* Augustine had expressed the same doctrinal understanding.

> And all my hope is no where but in Thy exceeding great mercy. Give what Thou enjoinest, and enjoin what Thou wilt. Thou enjoinest us continency; and *when I knew*, saith one, *that no man can be continent, unless God give it, this also was a part of wisdom to know whose gift she is* (Augustine n.d., 249).

Thus total depravity in terms of Edwardsean moral inability did not excuse men from moral accountability to God's law; on the contrary, it only pointed out their need for the Mediator by whose virtue and obedience alone, through the faith that unites the sinner with him, the depraved sinner might be justified by a holy God with accompanying works of obedience as evidence of faith (Edwards 1879, 1:622-54).

Edwards affirmed the unconditional election doctrine on the following grounds:

> If God disposes all events, so that the infallible existence of the events is decided by his providence, then, doubtless, he thus orders and decides things *knowingly*, and on *design*. God does not do what he does, nor order what he orders,

> accidentally and unawares; either *without*, or *beside* his intention. And if there be a foregoing *design* of doing and ordering as he does, this is the same with a *purpose* or a *decree* (1879, 1:88).

The doctrine of limited atonement followed logically from unconditional election.

> However Christ in some sense may be said to *die for all*, and to redeem all visible Christians, yea, the whole world, by his death; yet there must be something *particular* in the design of his death, with respect to such as he intended should actually be saved thereby. As appears by what has been shown, God has the actual salvation or redemption of a certain number in his proper absolute design, and of a certain number only; and therefore such a design only can be prosecuted in any thing God does, in order to the salvation of men (1879, 1:88).

Edwards similarly endorsed the doctrine of irresistible grace "if by irresistible is meant, that which is attended with a moral necessity, which is impossible should ever be violated by any resistance" (1879, 1:87). John Bunyan in his sermon on John 6:37 entitled *Come and Welcome to Jesus Christ* had emphasized in his folksy style the irresistible grace contained in Christ's promise, "All that the Father gives me will come to me."

> If they *shall-come*, they *shall-come*; and he that hath said they *shall-come*, if faith and repentance be the *way* to come, as indeed they are, then faith and repentance *shall* be given to them for *shall-come* must be fulfilled on them (1979, 282).

> An absolute promise hath all the *conditional* ones in the belly of it, and also provision to answer all those qualifications, that *they* propound to him that seeketh for their benefits (Bunyan 1979, 283).

Though more metaphysical in style than Bunyan, Edwards shared Bunyan's theological affinity with the canons of Dort. Edwards's doctrine of the perseverance of the saints followed logically from the other points of Calvinism.

> If the beginning of true faith and holiness, and a man becoming a true saint at first, does not depend on the

self-determining power of the Will, but on the determining efficacious grace of God; it may well be argued, that it is also with respect to men being continued saints, or persevering in faith and holiness (1879, 1:88).

Edwards related the doctrine of perseverance to justification by faith.

> God, in the act of justification, which is passed on a sinner's first believing, has respect to perseverance, as being virtually contained in the first act of faith; and it is looked upon, and taken by him that justifies, as being as it were a property in that faith. God has respect to the believer's continuance in faith, and he is justified by that, as though it already were, because by divine establishment it shall follow; and it being by divine constitution connected with that first faith, as much as if it were a property in it, it is then considered as such, and so justification is not suspended; but were it not for this, it would be needful that it should be suspended, till the sinner had actually persevered in faith (1879, 1:641).

Neoplatonistic Tendencies

It may be seen from the foregoing section that the "theological objectivism" which had so characterized the writings of Edwards was Calvinistic in nature, as Holbrook himself acknowledged (Holbrook 1973, 4-5). Holbrook, however, insisted that Edwards's theological objectivism shed its Calvinistic frame in *True Virtue* and *The End for Which God Created the World* when his concept of Being took on monistic or panentheistic tendencies, "from which he escaped only by his continued differentiation between the subject and Object" (1973, 6). John Gerstner insisted that Edwards was "pantheistic by implication and panentheistic by intention" (1976, 99-107; Lesser 1981, 344-45). Cherry himself conceded that "a Neoplatonic metaphysic" employed by Edwards was at least suggestive of a monism in which uncreated and created being were not always properly differentiated (Cherry [1966] 1974, 86). Holbrook, Gerstner and Cherry most certainly had in mind Edwards's frequent use of the term "being in general." It was pointed out in the previous chapter that Edwards did, however, define his terms.

"Being in general" was defined as the system "comprehending the sum total of universal existence, both Creator and creature" (Edwards

1879, 1:98). For the sake of correcting the metaphysicians of his day Edwards employed a metaphysical term which established "existence" as a point of commonality or identification between Creator and creature. He did this, however, for the express purpose of differentiating between Creator and creature on the basis of "share of existence." Edwards's purpose was to demonstrate the "infinite" distance between Creator and the sum total of creatures, or between the "Being of beings" and the sum total of created existence, in order to counter those who regarded the sum total of the creatures as the *end* of their metaphysical system (Edwards 1879, 1:137-38).

> To determine then, what proportion of regard is to be allotted to the Creator, and all his creatures taken together, both must be as it were put in the balance; the *Supreme Being*, with all in him that is great and excellent, is to be compared with all that is to be found in the *whole creation*: and according as the former is found to outweigh, in such proportion is he to have a greater share of regard. And in this case, . . . the whole system of created beings, in comparison of the Creator, would be found as the light dust of the balance, or even as nothing and vanity (Edwards 1879, 1:98).

Having established the infinite distance between Creator and creation, with respect to proportion of existence and excellence, Edwards then proceeded to draw a comparison with respect to *degree* of proper regard on the basis of "actions and proceedings, determinations and effects whatever, whether creating, preserving, using, disposing, changing, or destroying." On this basis God came out the winner again--and by an infinite landslide margin!

> As the Creator is infinite, and has all possible existence, perfection, and excellence, so he must have all possible regard. As he is every way the first and supreme, and as his excellency is in all respects the supreme beauty and glory, the original good, and fountain of all good; so he must have in all respects the supreme regard. And as he is *God over all*, to whom all are properly subordinate, and on whom all depend, worthy to reign as supreme Head, with absolute and universal dominion; so it is *fit* that he should be so regarded by all, and in all proceedings and effects through the whole system (1879, 1:98).

In the *Nature of True Virtue* Edwards stated that God had "infinitely the greatest share of existence."

> So that all other being, even the whole universe, is as nothing in comparison of the Divine Being (1879, 1:125).

While Edwards defined virtue as "consent to being in general," he made it very clear that because of the infinite distance between God and his creation with respect to existence and excellence, such a consent to "being in general" was nothing less than "to love God supremely" (1879, 1:126-27).

> Yea, if there could be a cause determining a person to benevolence towards the whole world of mankind, or even all created sensible natures throughout the universe, exclusive of union of heart to general existence and of love to God--not derived from that temper of mind which disposes to a supreme regard to him, nor subordinate to such divine love--it cannot be the nature of true virtue (Edwards 1879, 1:136).

As Cherry pointed out, Edwards, consistent with Calvin, was careful to portray regeneration as a union of the human heart with God as opposed to a metaphysical absorption into, or identification with, the Being of God whereby the soul lost its own created identity or became a part of Deity.

> At any rate, there is in Edwards's thought and own life no manifest attempt to absorb man into the divine in "mystical" identity (Cherry [1966] 1974, 87).

Edwards's desire to be beatifically "swallowed up" in God had arisen from the truth of Scripture penetrating his heart and mind. The description of his beatific sensations was structured with solid doctrinal content which emphasized God's sovereignty in the salvation experience. For Edwards, Cherry said, "'Spiritual inwardness'" never replaced the "visible means of grace" or the "outward orientation of faith," but rather complemented these aspects. On the basis of these objective elements in Edwards's life and doctrine, this writer agrees with Cherry's conclusion in the matter: "One had best leave the mantle of 'mysticism' for another wearer than Edwards, for it fits him loosely at best" ([1966] 1974, 88).

As for the charge of "monistic" or "panentheistic" tendencies, it is quite apparent from a careful and honest study of *The End for Which God Created the World* and *The Nature of True Virtue* that there was no confusion in Edwards's mind regarding the infinite distance between the Creator and the creation, notwithstanding the analogous point of "existence." The creature's share of existence was as "nothing" when weighed on the scale opposite Deity. It should be apparent to the student of Scripture that the message which Edwards was sending to the secular metaphysicians and moral philosophers of his day was that which Isaiah had spoken:

> Surely the nations are like a drop in a bucket;
> They are regarded as dust on the scales. . . .
> Before him all the nations are as nothing;
> They are regarded by him as worthless and less than nothing.
> To whom, then, will you compare God? (Isaiah 40:15a, 17-18a NIV)

Edwards, it is true, united Creator and creation together in the single metaphysical category "being in general"; and then, in the next breath, he put infinite distance between the Supreme Being and created existence. In so doing, he was essentially saying in the language of metaphysics and moral philosophy what the Apostle Paul had said in the language of the Greek philosophers of his day: "'For in him we live and move and have our being'" (Act 17:28 NIV). If the Apostle John could make a christological appeal to the Greek mind, as well as to the Jewish, on the basis of the *logos* (John 1:1), Edwards would make a theological appeal to the secular philosophers of his day on the basis of "being." Edwards had his scriptural precedent just as John had had (Exod 3:14; John 8:58; Ps 33:6).

It might not be too far from the mark to say that Edwards used the language of psychological empiricism in *Religious Affections* and incorporated the metaphysical language of Neoplatonism in *The End for Which God Created the World* and *The Nature of True Virtue*, but that he filled the idioms, in both cases, with theological content consistent with Calvin. A poignant example of Edwards's use of Neoplatonist language for a theological purpose is the following excerpt from *The End for Which God Created the World*:

> We must conclude that such an arbitrator as I have supposed, would determine, that the whole universe in all its actings, proceedings, revolutions, and entire series of events, should proceed with a view to *God* as the supreme and last end; and that every wheel, in all its rotations, should move with a constant invariable regard to him as the ultimate end of all; as perfectly and uniformly, as if the whole system were animated and directed by one common soul (1879, 1:98).

Superficially, one might note Edwards's reference in the above quotation to "the whole system" being "animated and directed by one common soul" and conclude that Edwards's theology was pervaded by the Neoplatonist concept of a "world-soul" which Shaftesbury seemed to hold (Walker [1918] 1959, 98; Shaftesbury 1963, vol. 1, p. xxix-xxx). The fact is, however, that Edwards, after demonstrating the infinite superiority of the Creator with regard to *existence* and *excellence*, was stating on that basis that it would be fitting for the entire universe to submit to God's authority and purpose just as if God were the soul of the universe. Edwards was not endorsing the world-soul concept in the Neoplatonist sense, but simply affirming that the universe "should" recognize "*God*" as "the supreme and last end" and then the "system" would function as "perfectly and uniformly" as the one idealized by the Neoplatonists. A careful study of the quotation in context will show, in this writer's judgment, that this was the clear intention of Edwards's statement.

Finally, in regard to the "monistic" and "panentheistic" charge, Edwards's writings must be taken as a whole. It was noted in the previous chapter that Samuel Hopkins originally published *The End for Which God Created the World* and *The Nature of True Virtue* in a single volume as *Two Dissertations* (Murray 1987, 449). Just as *True Virtue* cannot be properly appreciated or understood in isolation from *God's End*, it may also be said that these two works must be interpreted in the context of Edwards's other writings, including *Original Sin, Freedom of the Will, Religious Affections, History of Redemption*, and *Justification by Faith*. If ever there were men given to synthetic thought, Edwards was one of them. Just prior to his death he revealed plans for a major treatise which was to embrace the whole of theology in relation to the history of redemption concluding with a consideration of "the perfect state of things" (Winslow [1940] 1979, 309-310).

> His mind could not rest until he had brought the whole system within his ken, and unified, it by a single idea (Winslow [1940] 1979, 327).

In view of Edwards's synthesizing pattern of thinking, it is imperative that his writings be studied as a whole. Furthermore, chapter 2 of this book has demonstrated that Edwards's writings must also be studied within the context of his philosophical milieu in order to understand and appreciate his unique employment of terms to convey Christian Truth.

When examined in this manner, the *Two Dissertations* which Samuel Hopkins originally had published as parts of a whole need not be viewed as having been stripped of their Calvinistic underpinnings, however their framework or form be considered.

It is also worthy of mention that Terrence Erdt, author of *Jonathan Edwards: Art and a Sense of the Heart*, traced Edwards's "sense of the heart, sweetness, and excellency" to the writings of John Calvin (Lesser 1981, 354, 361; Erdt 1980).

Covenantal Structure

Carl Bogue in his *Jonathan Edwards and the Covenant of Grace* demonstrated conclusively not only that Edwards was a Calvinist, but that "consistently with his Calvinism and his understanding of Scripture" he affirmed the essential elements of covenant theology (Bogue 1975, 306).

Perry Miller erred on at least two counts with respect to the matter of covenant theology. First of all, Miller stated that covenant theology was developed as a means to correct deficiencies in the Calvinistic doctrine of divine sovereignty in order to face the challenge of Arminianism and antinomianism.

> As controversy spread from the church to doctrine, Puritans had to defend their position not only against Anglicans but against two revolts within their own camp, against what was

> known at the time as "Arminianism" and against what for the sake of convenience we may call "Antinomianism." Both these errors sprang from orthodox Calvinism, both ended by repudiating certain fundamental doctrines, and both were driven to their conclusions by a sense of Calvinism's deficiencies ([1939] 1982, 367).

> If Arminianism resulted from a feeling that Calvin[ism] was deficient in ethical sanctions, Antinomianism came from a conviction that it did not go far enough with the doctrine of assurance ([1939] 1982, 370).

> The group of Puritans who made up the federal school endeavored to forestall Arminians and Antinomians by their doctrine of the Covenant of Grace, believing it no essential alteration of orthodox theology but a legitimate extension of its implication. The intellectual history of the century was to prove them sadly mistaken, and their imposition of the covenant doctrine upon the system of Calvin produced at last in the New England theology an altogether different philosophy from any propounded in Geneva ([1939] 1982, 367).

Miller contradicted his own thesis by acknowledging its anachronism in that the antinomian issue did not arise until well after the full-fledged development of the covenant theological scheme.

> It is not quite accurate to look upon the Covenant as a direct reply to Arminians and Antinomians; ambiguities inherent in the doctrines of sanctification and assurance would have forced theologians to rethink them in any event, and the covenant theory developed in England before Antinomianism became a great concern ([1939] 1982, 371).

If Miller's own self-contradiction was not sufficient to invalidate his own thesis concerning the origin of covenant theology, a simple glance at the New England antinomian controversy, 1636-38, would have sufficed. Anne Hutchinson followed John Cotton to Massachusetts Bay having become enamored of his teachings on the covenant of grace. She became the focal point of the antinomian controversy which nearly ruined the "holy commonwealth." Hutchinson, who was banished from Massachusetts Bay by the General Court in November, 1637, and excommunicated from the Boston Church in March, 1638, had (among other things) judged all Massachusetts Bay pastors, with the exception of two, as being under a "covenant of works." As was noted in chapter 1, Hutchinson insisted that sanctification was not an essential evidence of justification thereby threatening the "visible saints" structure of the "holy commonwealth" (Hall 1968; Higgins 1984, 1:195-273).

Two observations may be made on the antinomian controversy that invalidate Perry Miller's thesis: (1) the antinomian controversy arose, not merely from within Calvinism, but from within the New England Puritan state where the covenant concept was the matrix of theology (as well as politics); therefore Miller's own acknowledgment of an anachronism in his thesis is clearly substantiated; and (2) that the antinomian issue could arise in such monstrous proportions, within a "covenantal" setting, demonstrates the tenuous basis for Miller's thesis that covenant theology was developed to overcome a deficiency in Calvinism in order to combat more effectively the error of antinomianism. Whatever strength the covenantal structure gave to Calvinism was sufficient neither to prevent antinomianism's occurrence, nor to prevent it from pleading its seditious cause in the guise of covenant theology. Hutchinson had simply cloaked her antinomianism in the garb of the covenant of grace and castigated all challengers as being under the bondage of a covenant of works. Thus, Perry Miller's thesis cannot be taken seriously.

An alternative to Miller's thesis was suggested by Miller himself and that was the "Puritan" thesis--simply that "the doctrine of the Covenant of Grace" represented "no essential alteration of orthodox theology" but was "a legitimate extension of its implication" ([1939] 1982, 367). Peter A. Lillback, in his brilliant dissertation "The Binding of God: Calvin's Role in the Development of Covenant Theology" (1985), documented the explicit covenantal elements in John Calvin's theology which had even broader implications for a much more developed covenant theology based on Calvin's thought. He noted no less than 273 references in Calvin's works to Latin words which were translatable into English as "covenant" (Letham 1986). Lillback's seminal work would suggest, therefore, that covenant theology was a "legitimate extension" of Calvin's thought, rather than an "imposition" upon Calvin, as Miller had charged. This was Carl Bogue's conclusion as well when he stated that Jonathan Edwards taught the covenant of grace "consistently with his Calvinism" (1975, 306).

If the first error Miller made respecting covenant theology had to do with its origin, Miller's second error was his suggestion that Jonathan Edwards had repudiated covenant theology. Referring to Edwards's Boston Public Lecture of 1731, Miller stated, "The Federal Theology is conspicuous in his sermon by its utter absence ([1949] 1973, 30). In reference to "Edwards's discourses on justification, which reverberated through the land even before they were published," Miller said, "The scandal . . . was his rejection of the covenant" ([1949] 1973, 115-16; Bogue 1975, 89).

If Edwards's theology did represent a repudiation of covenant theology, it would be strange indeed, for, as Perry Miller himself acknowledged, New England Puritan thought was a unified system, and three of the men who were the system's chief architects were covenant theologians (Miller [1939] 1982, vii). Quoting from Miller's *New England Mind: The Seventeenth Century*, Carl Bogue measured the impact of these three men upon colonial New England.

> Though these men never set foot in America, they exerted so deep and pervasive an influence upon the colonial intellect that their books must be treated to all intents and purposes as though they were productions of that intellect. . . . Three great teachers in particular were responsible for much of the New England creed: William Perkins, William Ames, and John Preston (Bogue 1975, 74).

John E. Eusden, in his introduction to Ames's *Marrow of Theology*, noted that Ames's work had been standard reading for undergraduates at Harvard and Yale and that Edwards in particular had obtained a copy of the 1634 edition, "twice signed it and added notes which bespeak his indebtedness" (Ames [1629] 1983, 1-2).

> Jonathan Edwards (1703-58) often began with the thought of the Franeker professor. In early American theological and intellectual history, William Ames was without peer (Ames [1629] 1983, 11).

In setting forth the "Application of Christ," Ames had postulated the doctrine of the eternal covenant of redemption that transpired between the Father and the Son. He had stated that the "application" of Christ's work by the Holy Spirit depended first of all, "upon the

Father's decree and donation," secondly, "upon the intention of Christ," and thirdly, "upon the acceptance of the Father."

> 3. The agreement between God and Christ was a kind of advance application of our redemption and deliverance of us to our surety and our surety to us. Upon that latter redemption, to be completed in us, it has the effect of a kind of efficacious example; the former is a representative of the latter and the latter is brought into being by the former.
> 4. Thus our deliverance from sin and death was not only determined by the decree of God but also granted and communicated to Christ and to us in him before it was known by us ([1629] 1983, 149).

In consideration of Edwards's theological "indebtedness" to men such as Williams Ames, one should not be surprised that Edwards expressed the same concept of the covenant of redemption. It might come as a surprise, however, that this would be so clearly set forth in Edwards's discourse on *Justification by Faith* in regard to which Miller had stated "The scandal . . . was his rejection of the covenant" ([1949] 115-16).

> There was a transaction between the Father and the Son, that was antecedent to Christ's becoming man, and being made under the law, wherein he undertook to put himself under the law, and both to obey and to suffer; in which transaction these things were already virtually done in the sight of God; as is evident by this, that God acted on the ground of that transaction, justifying and saving sinners, as if the things undertaken had been actually performed long before they were performed indeed (1879, 1:637).

In the *History of Redemption* Edwards set forth this same eternal covenantal design.

> Some things were done before the world was created, yea from eternity. The persons of Trinity were, as it were, confederated in a design, and a covenant of redemption. In this covenant the Father had appointed the Son, and the Son had undertaken the work; and all things to be accomplished in the world were stipulated and agreed. There were things done at the *creation* of the world, in order to that work; for the world itself seems to have been created in order to it (1879, 1:534).

Edwards clearly subordinated the work of creation to the covenant of redemption. In his synthesizing manner, Edwards in *God's End in Creation*, went a step further relating redemption to the highest theme of Scripture--the glory of God.

> It is manifest from Scripture, that God's glory is the last end of that great work of providence, the work of *redemption* by Jesus Christ (1879, 1:110).

If the basis for Edwards's rejection of Arminianism and acceptance of the five points of Calvinism was his regard for the glory of God, so it was also noteworthy that his view of the covenantal scheme issued necessarily and supremely in the glory of God.

Edwards's concept of the "covenant of grace" was simply "the historical implementation of the eternal covenant of redemption" (Bogue 1975, 113).

> The various dispensations or works that belong to it, are but the several parts of one scheme. It is but one design that is formed, to which all the offices of Christ directly tend, and in which all the persons of the Trinity conspire. All the various dispensations that belong to it are united; and the several wheels are one machine, to answer one end, and produce one effect (Edwards 1879, 1:534).

The covenant of grace or, in Bogue's words, the "historical implementation of the eternal covenant of redemption," was for Edwards "the external covenant" (1879, 1:534). This externalizing of the eternal covenant Edwards described in the following way in *God's End in Creation*:

> It appears reasonable to suppose, that it was God's last end, that there might be a glorious and abundant emanation of his infinite fulness of good *ad extra*, or without himself; and that the disposition to communicate himself, or diffuse his own FULNESS, was what moved him to create the world.

In a footnote, Edwards defined his terms:

> I shall often use the phrase *God's fulness*, as signifying and comprehending all the good which is in God natural and

> moral, either excellence or happiness: partly, because I knew of no better phrase to be used in this general meaning; and partly, because I am led hereto by some of the inspired writers, particularly the Apostle Paul, who often useth the phrase in this sense (1879, 1:100).

In reference to Edwards's *History of the Work of Redemption*, which consisted of a series of sermons preached in 1739 and represented a draft for Edwards's proposed *Summa*, Carl Bogue commented,

> So central is the covenant of grace to this work one could almost substitute the title of "A History of the Covenant of Grace" (1975, 117).

The accuracy of Bogue's comment is attested by Edwards's introductory remarks in which he set forth the covenantal design for the events he was about to describe.

> In all this God designed to accomplish the glory of the blessed Trinity in an eminent degree. God had a design of glorifying himself from eternity; yea, to glorify each person in the Godhead. The *end* must be considered as first in the order of nature, and then the means; and therefore we must conceive, that God having professed this end, had then as it were the means to choose; and the principal means that he adopted was this great work of redemption (1879, 1:536).

Edwards viewed the covenant of grace as commencing immediately after the Fall.

> I. As soon as man fell, Christ entered on his mediatorial work. Then it was that he began to execute the work and office of a mediator. He had undertaken it before the world was made. He stood engaged with the Father to appear as man's mediator, and to take on that office when there should be occasion, from all eternity. But now the time was come. . . . He immediately stepped in between a holy, infinite, offended Majesty, and offending mankind. . . .
> II. Presently upon this the gospel was first revealed on earth, in these words, Gen.iii.15. "And I will put enmity between thee and the woman, and between thy seed and her seed: it shall bruise thy head, and thou shalt bruise his heel." . . . In those words of God there was an intimation of another surety to be appointed for man, after the first surety had

> failed. This was the first revelation of the covenant of grace; the first dawning of the light of the gospel on earth (1879, 1:536-37).

Edwards viewed the Flood at the time of Noah as a further unfolding, or manifestation, of the covenant of grace (Bogue 1975, 118).

> And therefore, God's destroying those enemies of the church by the flood belongs to this affair of redemption; for it was one thing that was done in fulfillment of the covenant of grace, as it was revealed to *Adam*: "I will put enmity between thee and the woman, and between thy seed and her seed; it shall bruise thy head." This was only a destruction of the seed of the serpent in the midst of their most violent rage against the seed of the woman, when in the utmost peril by them (1879, 1:541).

Bogue noted Edwards's repeated references to God's confirmations of the covenant of grace with Abraham (1975, 119-21). Especially striking was the following reference in *Qualifications for Communion* which depicted the Abrahamic covenant as an expression of the covenant of grace:

> Indeed the main thing, the substance and marrow of that covenant which God made with Abraham and the other patriarchs, was the *covenant of grace*, which is continued in these days of the gospel, and extends to all his spiritual seed, of the Gentiles as well as Jews: but yet that covenant with the patriarchs contained other things that were appendages to that everlasting covenant of grace; promises of lesser matters, subservient to the grand promise of the future seed, and typical of things appertaining to him. Such were those that annexed the blessing to the land of Canaan, and the progeny of Isaac and Jacob (1879, 1:462).

Edwards continued, citing the Davidic covenant as a further development of the covenant of grace.

> Just so it was also as to the covenant God made with David. 2 Sam. vii. and Psal. cxxxii. If we consider that covenant with regard to its marrow and soul, it was the covenant of grace: but there were other subservient promises which were typical of its benefits; such were promises of blessings to the nation of Israel, of continuing the temporal crown to David's posterity, and of fixing the blessing to Jerusalem or Mount

> Zion, as the place where he chose to set his name there. And in this sense it was that the *very family* of Jacob were *God's people by covenant*, and his *chosen people*; even when they were no visible saints, when they lived in idolatry, and made no profession of the true religion. . . .
>
> God's covenant with Abraham is in some sense in force with respect to that people, and reaches them even to this day; and yet surely they are not God's covenant people, in the sense that visible Christians are. See Lev. xxvi.42 (1879, 462-63).

Edwards cited Isaiah 55:1-3 as evidence that the Davidic covenant was an expression of the covenant of grace (Bogue 1975, 122). In speaking of the covenant of grace in this way, Edwards was endorsing Calvin as well, as the following excerpts from the *Institutes* will show:

> The Lord of old willed that his people direct and elevate their minds to the heavenly heritage; yet, to nourish them better in this hope, he displayed it for them to see and, so to speak, taste, under earthly benefits. But now that the gospel has more plainly and clearly revealed the grace of the future life, the Lord leads our minds to meditate upon it directly, laying aside the lower mode of training that he used with the Israelites (1960, 1:450).
>
> *The earthly promises corresponded to the childhood of the church in the Old Covenant; but were not to chain hope to earthly things* (1960, 1:451).
>
> The second difference between the Old and New Testaments consists in figures: that, in the absence of the reality, it showed but an image and shadow in place of the substance; the New Testament reveals the very substance of truth as present (1960, 1:453).
>
> The fifth difference . . . lies in the fact that until the advent of Christ, the Lord set apart one nation within which to confine the covenant of his grace (1960, 1:460).

While acknowledging certain elements of antithesis between law and gospel, Calvin, like Edwards, stressed the underlying *continuity* between the Testaments. "Ours distinguishes between the clarity of the gospel and the obscurer dispensation of the Word that had preceded it" (1960, 1:459). "Where the whole law is concerned, the gospel differs from it only in clarity of manifestation" (1960, 1:427).

> God has never manifested himself to men in any other way than through the Son, that is, his sole wisdom, light, and truth. From this fountain Adam, Noah, Abraham, Isaac, Jacob, and others drank all that they had of the heavenly teaching (1960, 2:1153).
>
> The gospel did not so supplant the entire law as to bring forward a different way of salvation. Rather, it confirmed and satisfied whatever the law had promised, and gave substance to the shadows (1960, 1:427).

Another distinguishing feature of covenant theology was the concept of a covenant of works originally established with Adam prior to the Fall and later amplified at Sinai. William Ames spoke of it in the *Marrow of Theology*.

> 9. From this special way of governing rational creatures there arises a covenant between God and them. This covenant is, as it were, a kind of transaction of God with the creature whereby God commands, promises, threatens, fulfills; and the creature binds himself in obedience to God so demanding ([1629] 1983, 111).

Ames had been careful to point out that the covenant was not between equals "but between lord and servant." Furthermore,

> in this covenant the moral deeds of the intelligent creature lead either to happiness as a reward or to unhappiness as a punishment. The latter is deserved, the former not ([1629] 1983, 111).

Ames stated that "in substance" this was "the same law as the moral law of the decalogue." This law was given to Adam as a "public person or the head of the family of man" ([1629] 1983, 111, 113).

The Westminster Confession, to which Edwards subscribed, had embodied the covenant of works (Murray 1987, 346; Rolston 1972, 15-20).

> I. The distance between God and the creature is ever so great, that although reasonable creatures do owe obedience unto Him as their Creator, yet they could never have any fruition of Him as their blessedness and reward, but by some

> voluntary condescension on God's part, which He hath been pleased to express by way of covenant.
>
> II. The first covenant made with man was a covenant of works, wherein life was promised to Adam; and in him to his posterity, upon condition of perfect and personal obedience.
>
> III. Man, by his fall, having made himself uncapable of life by that covenant, the Lord was pleased to make a second, commonly called the covenant of grace (Committee n.d., chap. VII).
>
> I. God gave to Adam a law, as a covenant of works, by which He bound him and all his posterity to personal, entire, exact, and perpetual obedience, promised life upon the fulfilling, and threatened death upon the breach of it, and endued him with power and ability to keep it.
>
> II. This law, after his fall, continued to be a perfect rule of righteousness; and, as such, was delivered by God upon Mt. Sinai, in ten commandments, and written in two tables.
> . . .
> VI. Although true believers be not under the law, as a covenant of works, to be thereby justified, or condemned; yet is it of great use to them, as well as to others (Committee n.d., chap. XIX).

Edwards significantly predicated *Original Sin* upon the covenant of works as set forth in Ames's *Marrow* and later in the Westminster Confession.

> God, in every step of his proceeding with Adam, in relation to the covenant or constitution established with him, looked on his posterity as being *one with him* (1879, 1:220).

> God, in his constitution with Adam, dealt with him as a *public person*--as the head of the human species--and had respect to his posterity as included in him. And it must appear, that this history is given by divine revelation . . . in order to exhibit to our view the origin of the present sinful, miserable state of mankind, that we might see what that was, which first gave occasion for all those consequent wonderful dispensations of divine mercy and grace towards mankind, which are the great subject of the Scriptures, both of the Old and New Testament (1879, 1:187).

In keeping with the design both of Ames and the Westminster Confession, Edwards viewed the moral law given at Mt. Sinai as a further expression of the covenant of works.

> The covenant of works was here exhibited as a schoolmaster to lead to Christ, not only for the use of that nation, under the Old Testament, but for the use of God's church throughout all ages of the world. It is an instrument that the great Redeemer makes use of to convince men of their sin, misery, and helpless state, and of God's awful and tremendous majesty and justice as a lawgiver, in order to make men sensible of the necessity of Christ as a Savior. This work of redemption, in its saving effect on men's souls, in all its progress, is not carried on without the use of the law at Mt. Sinai (1879, 1:547).

As evident from Edwards's foregoing statements, regarding both the Adamic and Sinaitic expressions of the covenant of works, the covenant of works was clearly subordinate to, and subservient to, the work of redemption (i.e., the covenant of grace). It was also apparent that the Sinaitic moral law, in its function as a covenant of works, corresponded to the first use of the law which Calvin had described: "*The law shows the righteousness of God, and as a mirror discloses our sinfulness, leading us to implore divine help*" (Calvin 1960, 1:354). John Cotton had described the Sinaitic law in its function as a covenant of works in much the same way.

> Thus he dealt with the Children of *Israel* and called them to be a singular people unto himselfe, and yet but in a Covenant of works, Deut 7.6, 7, 8. Thus doth the Lord deale with all those whom he receiveth to be a people unto himself; and by this spirit of bondage he draweth them from all their sinful lusts and passions, so as that they can find no hope or mercy in anything; and as this is properly a Seal of the Covenant of works, as the Spirit of Adoption is a Seal of the Covenant of Grace. Rom 8.15 (Cotton 1654, 20)

> As a School-master driveth his Scholar through fear, unto this or that duty; so the Law of God driveth the soul through fear unto *Jesus Christ*; not that it doth reveal *Christ* a Savior and Redeemer of Free Grace, but the soul being once brought down under the sense of sin by the terrors of the *Law*, will readily and diligently hearken unto the news of Christ a Savior: for being once sensible of his own inability to redeem himself, and unworthiness to be redeemed from the wrath of God, now is the Soul fitted to hear the voice of the Gospell, now is the news of Jesus Christ beautiful, and glad tidings: and of this use is the *Law* unto the *Elect* of God, before they come under the Covenant of the Grace of God (1671, 69).

The Westminster Confession, it was noted, had also regarded the Sinaitic law as a "perfect rule of righteousness" of "great use" to "true believers." This was consistent with Calvin's third use of the law: "*Principally it admonishes believers and urges them on in well-doing.*"

> Here is the best instrument for them to learn more thoroughly each day the nature of the Lord's will to which they aspire, and to confirm them in the understanding of it (Calvin 1960, 1:360).

Edwards, similarly, recognized this use of the Sinaitic moral law as a "rule of righteousness" in the lives of believers.

> And it was a great thing, whether we consider it as a new exhibition of the covenant of works, or given as a rule of life. . . .
> If we regard the law given at Mount Sinai--not as a covenant of works, but--as a rule of life, it is employed by the Redeemer, from that time to the end of the world, as a directory to his people, to show them the way in which they must walk, as they would go to heaven: for a way of sincere and universal obedience to this law is the narrow way that leads to life (1879, 1:547, 548).

Edwards developed his discourse on *Justification by Faith* in reference to the Adamic Covenant of works whereby he set forth Christ as the second Adam (or federal head).

> Christ by suffering the penalty, and so making atonement for us, only removes the guilt of our sins, and so sets us in the same state that Adam was in the first moment of creation: and it is no more fit that we should obtain eternal life only on that account, than that Adam should have the reward of eternal life, or of a confirmed and unalterable state of happiness, the first moments of his existence, without any obedience at all. Adam was not to have the reward merely on account of his being innocent. . . .
> So on the same account we have not eternal life merely as void of guilt, which we have by the atonement of Christ; but on the account of Christ's activeness in obedience, and doing well. Christ is our second federal head, and is called the second Adam, 1 Cor. xv.22. because he acted that part for us which Adam should have done. . . .

> As if Adam had persevered, and finished his course of obedience, we should have received the benefit of his obedience, as much as now we have the mischief of his disobedience; so in like manner, there is reason that we should receive the benefit of the second Adam's obedience, as of his atonement of our disobedience (1879, 1:636-37).

In Edwards's view, Christ executed the covenant of grace as our Mediator by fulfilling the covenant of works as the second Adam, and this was a far more glorious thing than even if the first Adam had simply obeyed, even as redemption exceeds creation in splendor, and grace exceeds nature (see appendix).

> Christ, by subjecting himself to the law, and obeying it, has done great honour to the law, and to the authority of God who gave it. That so glorious a person should become subject to the law, and fulfil it, has done much more to honour it, than if mere man had obeyed it. It was a thing infinitely honourable to God, that a person of infinite dignity was not ashamed to call him his God, and to adore him and obey him as such. This was more to God's honour than if any mere creature, of any possible degree of excellence and dignity, had so done (1879, 1:636).

In his treatise on *Original Sin*, Edwards again insisted that Christ's obedience was far more glorious than Adam's could have been.

> For those that are saved by Christ, are not merely advanced to happiness by his merits, but saved from the infinitely dreadful effects of Adam's sin, and many from immense guilt, pollution, and misery, by personal sins. They are also brought to a holy and happy state through infinite obstacles; and exalted to a far greater degree of dignity, felicity, and glory, than would have been due for *Adam's* obedience (1879, 1:187).

Edwards adamantly opposed the Arminian scheme whereby justification consisted of forgiveness for past sins only and the believer was left to his own merit and effort for the efficacy of future moral acts. Edwards insisted on the necessity of Christ's "positive obedience, in order to his obtaining, as our second Adam, the reward of eternal life" (1879, 1:636). He stated,

> We are taught in Scripture that heaven is purchased for us;
> it is called a *purchased possession* Eph. i.14 (1879, 1:638).

It was not enough to pay a man's debt and set him at liberty in order that he might have opportunity to acquire an estate by his own effort.

> To suppose that all Christ does is only to make atonement for us by suffering, is to make him our Savior but in part. It is to rob him of half his glory as Savior. For if so, all that he does is to deliver us from hell; he does not purchase heaven for us (1879, 1:638).

The justification for which Christ was raised on our behalf included the reward of eternal life, and not merely acquittal coupled with a second chance (Edwards 1879, 1:637). To suppose that in any sense, or to any degree, man was justified by his own sincere obedience, virtue, or goodness, derogated from gospel grace.

> That scheme of justification that manifestly takes from or diminishes the grace of God, is undoubtedly to be rejected. . . . The Scripture teaches, that the way of justification appointed in the gospel-covenant is appointed for that end, that free grace might be expressed, and glorified; Rom. iv.16. "Therefore it is of faith, that it might be by grace." The exercising and magnifying of free grace in the gospel-contrivance for the justification and salvation of sinners, is evidently the chief design of it. And this freedom and riches of grace in the gospel is everywhere spoken of in Scripture as the chief glory of it (Edwards 1879, 1:635).

The "gospel-contrivance," of course, was the covenantal scheme entered into by the Father and the Son in the eternal counsel of the Godhead and implemented in the history of redemption. That such was the case was plainly evidenced by Edwards's use of the expression "gospel-covenant" in the same paragraph. Perhaps if Perry Miller had understood Edwards's use of the word "contrivance," he would not have stated that "Federal Theology," in Edwards's Boston Public Lecture, was "conspicuous by its absence"; nor could he have spoken of the "scandal" of Edwards's "rejection of the covenant" in *Justification by Faith* from which the above passage was quoted (Miller [1949] 1973, 30-31, 115-16). The "gospel-contrivance" which Edwards used interchangeably with "gospel-covenant," and which in his mind was consistent with Calvinism, was that which glorified God by establishing man's dependence. Such a scheme Edwards would embrace. If "the contrary scheme" of Arminianism was followed, not only did it re-establish the Adamic covenant of works (Edwards 1879, 1:652), but

> it utterly overthrows the glory of all the great things that have been contrived, and done, and suffered in the work of redemption. . . . It diminishes the glory of the grace of God and the Redeemer, and proportionably magnifies man. It makes the goodness and excellency of fallen man to be something, which I have shown are nothing (Edwards 1879, 1:653).

One of the major issues among those who espoused covenant theology was whether the covenant of grace was to be regarded as conditional or unconditional. To suggest that it was conditional seemed to re-introduce a covenant of works; contrarily, to speak of a covenant which was unconditional smacked of antinomianism.

John Cotton had emphasized the unilateral nature of the covenant of grace. He stated that it was the nature of the promises

> to direct us whither to look for qualifications, and the blessings promised unto them; namely, to the Lord Jesus Christ, to receive the blessing through him, and the qualification by the same hand; for they are first fulfilled in him; there is no good *Condition* but it is fulfilled in Jesus Christ, *no blessings* belonging thereunto, but it is found in Christ also (Cotton 1671, 61).

> Faith uniting us to Christ, is ever upon an absolute Promise; or a condition subsequent, not antecedent. If you will say it is a Promise to a condition, what kind of condition was it? There is no condition before Faith; for then a man is out of the way of any gracious Blessing from Heaven; no condition before it, whereby man can close with Jesus Christ: and if it was a condition after Faith, unto which the promise was made, the Faith was there before; and whatsoever followeth conversion, is no ground of Faith but a fruit and effect of it: Therefore I say, our first coming on to Christ, cannot be upon a conditional, but upon an absolute Promise (Cotton 1671, 37-38).

Cotton had been viewed with suspicion by the ministers of Massachusetts Bay because of his unwitting support of antinomian Anne Hutchinson. His statement before the Boston Conference did not even regard faith as a condition of justification.

> Faith may be stated to be passive in our justification because it doth not lay hold on Christ, to fetch Justification from him, till Christ have first laid hold on us, and imputed his righteousness to us, and declared it unto us by his Spirit, in a free promise of Grace; And then Faith becometh active, actually to receive Christ's righteousness; and actually to beleeve on it, either by way of dependence or assurance (Higgins 1984, 1:234).

In support of this position, Cotton summed up Calvin's description of faith in the *Institutes*:

> . . . a firm and sure knowledge of divine favor toward us, founded in the truth of a free promise in Christ, and revealed and sealed on our hearts, by the Holy Spirit (Higgins 1984, 1:236; Calvin 1960, 1:575).

Cotton distinguished between "actual" faith, or faith as "habit," and "active" faith, or faith as "act." Faith as "habit" was "grace" and the "formal cause" of justification. The Spirit of God was the "efficient cause," and faith as "act" was "instrument" but not "instrumental cause." Higgins noted that, for Cotton, justifying faith was not properly the "faith that justifies," but rather the "faith that reveals to an individual that he is justified." Cotton regarded "union" with Christ as antecedent to "justifying faith"; whereas most of the New England clergy regarded both faith as "habit" and faith as "act" as antecedent conditions of union with Christ (Higgins 1984, 1:163-65, 167, 169). The New England clergy were not in the same camp with the Arminians who ignored human depravity and regarded man's will as "efficient cause," but their position was clearly distinct from the unilateral view of faith espoused by Cotton (Higgins 1984, 1:153).

In articulating his views regarding the conditions of the covenant, Edwards was well aware of the danger of antinomianism on the one hand, and Arminianism on the other, as well as the inherent difficulty in the use of language.

> Here, if I may humbly express what seems evident to me, though faith be indeed the condition of justification so as nothing else is, yet this matter is not clearly and sufficiently explained by saying that faith is the condition of justification; and that because the word seems ambiguous, both in common use, and also as used in divinity (Edwards 1879, 1:623).

Edwards went on to say, as Cotton had, that in one sense Christ alone had performed the condition of justification and salvation; however, in another sense, faith was the condition. The problem, in Edwards's mind, was the precise definition of "condition."

> If it be that with which, or which being supposed, a thing shall be, and without which, or it being denied, a thing shall not be, we in such a case call it a condition of that thing. But in this sense faith is not the only condition of salvation or justification; for there are many things that accompany and flow from faith, with which justification shall be and without which it shall not be, and therefore are found to be put in Scripture in conditional propositions with justification and salvation . . .; such are love to God, and love to brethren, forgiving men their trespasses, and many other good qualifications and acts (1879, 1:623).

Edwards noted, "There is a difference between being justified by a thing, and that thing universally, necessarily, and inseparably attending justification" (1879, 1:623).

Edwards was less than satisfied with the Calvinistic definition of faith as *instrument*, which Cotton had endorsed, because of the injurious misrepresentation of those who charged the Calvinists with regarding faith as the instrument in God's hand. Edwards apparently wanted to steer clear of Cotton's antinomian tendencies and define faith as "act" rather than both "habit" and "act." Edwards knew that traditionally Calvinists, in using the word "instrument," had meant "the instrument wherein we receive justification."

> But yet, it must be owned, this is an obscure way of speaking, and there must certainly be some impropriety in calling it an instrument wherewith we receive or accept justification; for the very persons who thus explain the matter, speak of faith as being the reception or acceptance itself; and if so, how can it be the instrument of reception or acceptance? Certainly

there is a difference between the act and the instrument (1879, 1:624).

Edwards then proceeded to speak of the divine constitution of things whereby God, in view of the mediatorial work of Christ, regarded it "a fit thing" that the person who believed in Christ should be justified.

> The wisdom of God in his constitutions doubtless appears much in the fitness and beauty of them, so that those things are established to be done that are fit to be done, and that those things are connected in his constitution that are agreeable one to another (Edwards 1879, 1:624).

For Edwards, faith was simply a *"uniting act."*

> God does not give those that believe an union with or an interest in the Savior as a *reward* for faith, but only because faith is the soul's *active* uniting with Christ, or is itself the very act of unition, *on their part*. . . . God, in requiring this in order to an union with Christ as one of his people, treats men as reasonable creatures, capable of act and choice; and hence sees it fit that they only who are one with Christ by their own act, should be looked upon as one *in law*. What is *real* in the union between Christ and his people, is the foundation of what is *legal* (1879, 1:626).

When Edwards spoke of men's capability of "act and choice," he meant, of course, *natural* capability as distinct from *moral* capability (Edwards 1879, 1:10-12). Similarly when he spoke of the "fitness" or "congruity" between a person's faith in Christ and the person's justification by God, he made it clear that he was speaking of a *natural* fitness or congruity as distinct from *moral* fitness or congruity. There was no merit inherent in the faith act itself to establish moral congruity.

> A person has a natural fitness for a state, when it appears meet and condescent that he should be in such a state or circumstances, only from the natural concord or agreeableness there is between such qualifications and such circumstances; not because the qualifications are lovely or unlovely, but only because the qualifications and the circumstances are like one another, or do in their nature suit and agree or unite to another (1879, 1:627).

Edwards said that it was only on this latter account of natural fitness that

> he whose heart sincerely unites itself to Christ as his Savior, should be looked upon as united to that Savior, and so having an interest in him; and not from any moral fitness there is between the excellency of such a qualification as faith, and such a glorious blessedness as the having an interest in Christ (1879, 1:627).

Thus God's justification of the sinner on the basis of faith was simply a testimony to "God's love of order" (Edwards 1879, 1:627). Fiering observed that the concept of "fittingness" was prevalent in the writings of Adrian Heereboord (1613-1661) whose influence spread to Harvard through Charles Morton in the 1690s. He also noted its occurrence in the writings of Samuel Clark and Thomas Shepherd (Fiering 1981b, 96, 101; 1981a, Note, 90). Calvin himself had regarded it as a thing quite "unfitting" for a person to be assigned the "place and rank of children" who had not been "engrafted into the body of the only-begotten Son" (Calvin 1960, 1:342). However Edwards came by the concept of "fitness," he made thorough use of it (1879, 1:75, 98), and with regard to the matter of the covenantal conditions, it enabled him to steer clear of Arminianism while regarding faith as uniting *"act."*

From the foregoing summary and analysis of Edwards's Calvinistic and covenantal theology, it may be seen that for Edwards the issue was one with the object of beatific vision. Edwards could not escape the element of the transcendent glory of God. Whether he was addressing the issues raised by the benevolist moral philosophers, or the ones raised by the Arminians--it was all the same, the sum of the matter was the glory of God. Just as any scheme of moral philosophy that did not have the supreme love to God as its foundation was "fundamentally and essentially defective," so the Arminian scheme which made God dependent on man was to be rejected (1879, 1:127). The glory of God had been the Puritan issue from the beginning in New England. The corporate dream had been expounded by Winthrop on board the *Arbella*.

> We shall find that the God of Israel is among us, when ten of us shall be able to resist a thousand of our enemies, when He shall make us a praise and glory, that men shall say of

> succeeding plantations: "The Lord make it like that of New
> England." For we must consider that we shall be as a city on
> a hill, the eyes of all people are upon us (Miller [1956] 1982,
> 83).

New England, and the rest of America for that matter, would have to choose whether to define benevolence in terms of the secular priorities of the Cartesian Revolution or heed the cry of the last Puritan. Similarly they would have to choose between an Arminian salvation that exalted human freedom and one that glorified God in man's dependence. Their choice would not alter the ontological reality which the last Puritan was setting forth. It would, however, determine the nature of the city on the hill and the eternal destinies of her citizenry. To put it in Edwardsean terms, their choice would itself be determined by that motive which reigned supremely in their hearts--either the glory of God as evidence of grace, or self-interest as evidence of depravity according to the inscrutable righteous decree of the God of glory.

> God's absolute sovereignty and justice, with respect to
> salvation and damnation, is what my mind seems to rest
> assured of, as much as of any thing that I see with my eyes;
> at least it is so at times. But I have often since that first
> conviction, had quite another kind of sense of God's
> sovereignty than I had then. I have often since had not only
> a conviction, but a delightful conviction. The doctrine has
> very often appeared exceedingly pleasant, bright, and sweet.
> Absolute sovereignty is what I love to ascribe to God
> (Edwards 1879, vol. 1, p. lv).

CHAPTER V

BENEVOLENCE AND ARMINIANISM

Rationalist Arminian Benevolism

Conrad Wright, in *The Beginnings of Unitarianism in America*, stated,

> In taking a stand against the Great Awakening, Chauncy and the opposers had no idea that they were starting down the path to Arminianism. They thought they were defending the truths for which the first settlers had stood (1955, 56).

In 1739 George Whitefield's arrival in Philadelphia (his second visit to America) marked the beginning of an evangelistic preaching tour that was to set the colonies aflame with the revival fires of the Great Awakening. Regarded as the "Wonder of the Age," Whitefield selected an itinerary which took him to New York and then to the South where his ministry encountered the opposition of South Carolina's leading Anglican, Alexander Garden. (Whitefield, himself a Calvinist, had been ordained an Anglican and continued a member of the Church of England until his death.) Whitefield sailed from Charleston and on September 14, 1740 arrived in Newport, Rhode Island, where he preached twice in the Anglican Church. Moving on to Boston, he spent a week preaching at Brattle Street Church, Old South Church, the Boston Common (to a crowd of five thousand), First Church, Second Church, Harvard and again at First Church for the Thursday Public Lecture. He travelled as far north as Portsmouth and then returned to Boston and delivered a farewell message to thirty thousand people on the Common on October 12.

Whitefield proceeded to Northampton where he preached twice while Edwards wept. From there he moved on to New Haven and then to New York to conclude his six-week tour on October 29. Whitefield was impressed by the spiritual deadness of Harvard and Yale and of the American clergy in general, with the exception of Edwards and the Tennents.

Whitefield's preaching which focused on the "nature and necessity of the new birth" caused men to take sides. Thus the Great Awakening as epitomized by Whitefield and those who followed even more "enthusiastically" in his steps--most notably, Gilbert Tennent and James Davenport--would divide New England and the Presbyterians of the Middle Colonies into two camps. New England was divided into the Old Lights (those in opposition to the revival) and the New Lights (those in favor); the Presbyterians of the Middle Colonies, into the Old Side and New Side. In New England the Old Lights would be championed by Charles Chauncy who later became a Unitarian, and the New Lights united around the leadership of Jonathan Edwards (Ahlstrom 1972, 283-87; Heimert and Miller 1967, xxiv-xxix; Trinterud 1949, 86-108).

Conrad Wright, in assessing the effect of the Great Awakening upon New England, said,

> The effect of the revival was not so much to spread Arminianism as to prepare the way for its rapid growth. Down to the Awakening, a sense of community in New England still existed. . . . But after 1745, New England was so divided that there was a sense of community among the liberals and a sense of community among the evangelicals, but any wider sense of common purpose was wearing thin. Communication between the two groups increasingly took the form of debate, rather than the search for agreement; and the gap between the two widened rapidly. The opposers of 1745 were Arminian by 1755 (1955, 57-58).

Iain Murray significantly pointed out that the terms "liberal" and "Arminian" did not apply to Charles Chauncy at the beginning of his pastoral ministry. Chauncy had been ordained the same year as Edwards and served Boston's First Church as a colleague of the orthodox Benjamin Colman. Chauncy's initial opposition to the revival was related to the degree of emotionalism that was associated with it, as well as the perceived threat to the stability of the standing order from the infringement of itinerant ministries upon the established church parishes (Murray 1987, 281; Wright 1955, 39-41). This infringement of ministry frequently was attended with condemnatory pronouncements and insinuations of spiritual deadness among the established clergy. Gilbert Tennent's famous sermon, "The Danger of an Unconverted Ministry," was a major factor in the Old Side/New Side schism, and echoed overtones of much of the Great Awakening preaching (Heimert and Miller 1967, 71-99; Ahlstrom 1972, 271-74, 284-85; Trinterud 1949, 54-57).

The emotionalism which Chauncy despised came to its frenzied extreme in James Davenport, Yale graduate, pastor at Southold, Long Island, and great-grandson of New Haven's founder. Davenport's itinerant ministry in New England followed on the heels of Whitefield's and Tennent's. Judged mentally deranged at Hartford and at Boston, Davenport returned to New London, Connecticut, in March, 1743, where he organized a separatist church and had a book-burning ceremony including the works of men such as Flavel, Colman, and Increase Mather. Though he later was to issue his *Confessions and Retractions*, the damage had been done. Whitefield himself had been mildly reprimanded in private by Edwards for his "enthusiastical views." Chauncy's denunciation of the revival in his *Seasonable Thoughts on the State of Religion in New England* (1743) would single out Whitefield, Tennent, and Davenport, charging them with "enthusiasm" and "antinomianism." Edwards would respond with his *Treatise concerning Religious Affections* in 1746 (Ahlstrom 1972, 285-86, 302-3; Heimert and Miller 1967, chaps. 22 and 26; Winslow [1940] 1979, 186-87).

Norman Fiering traced the differences between Edwards and Chauncy to the moral philosophical debates of the previous century.

> It has not been adequately recognized that the divisions in American thought during the Great Awakening of the 1740's between evangelicals, so-called "Old Calvinists," and incipient liberal "Arminians" were partly a carry-over from the debates of the seventeenth century. . . . It is remarkable how close the

> correspondence is between the seventeenth-century Augustinian voluntarist position and the ideas of Jonathan Edwards, and between the seventeenth-century intellectualist position and the ideas of . . . Edwards's opponent, Charles Chauncy (1981b, 138).

Edwards insisted that practical intellect was not the sole determining factor of the will, but rather that the will was inclined according to the dominant motive which included the affections--loves and hates. *"True religion, in great part, consists in the affections"* (1879, 1:237). On the other hand Chauncy, in his *Seasonable Thoughts*, asked,

> Is it reasonable to think, that the *Divine Spirit*, in dealing with Men . . . would give their *Passions* the *chief* Sway over them? Would not this be to invert their Frame? . . . One of the most *essential* Things necessary in the *new-forming Men*, is the Reduction of their *Passions* to a proper Regimen, i.e. The Government of a *sanctified Understanding*. . . . *Reasonable* Beings are not to be guided by *Passion* or *Affection*, though the Object of it should be GOD. . . . The plain Truth is, an *enlightened Mind*, and not *raised Affections*, ought always to be the Guide of those who call themselves Men ([1743] 1975, 324, 325-6; Fiering 1981b, 142).

Chauncy clearly subordinated the affections to the intellect in his critique of the revival. Edwards responded,

> He that has doctrinal knowledge and speculation only, without affection, never is *engaged* in the business of religion (1879, 1:238).

> The Author of our nature has not only given us affections, but has made them very much the spring of actions (1879, 1:238).

> As there is no true religion where there is nothing else but affection, so there is no true religion where there is no *religious affection*. As on the one hand, there must be light in the understanding, as well as an *affected* fervent heart, or where there is heat without light, there can be nothing divine or heavenly in the heart: so, on the other hand, where there is a kind of light without heat, a head stored with notions and speculations with a cold and unaffected heart, there can be nothing divine in that light, that knowledge is no true spiritual

> knowledge of divine things. If the great things of religion are
> rightly understood, they will affect the heart (1879, 1:243).

Wright pointed out that though the revival was opposed at Yale, it was in the Harvard area that the opposition became entrenched and developed into Arminianism. Conversely, though there were evangelicals at Harvard, it was almost exclusively among Yale graduates where "increasing numbers of Edwardseans" could be found.

> In Boston, Charles Chauncy occupied a strategic position
> which made it possible for him to rally the forces of
> opposition to the revival as few of his colleagues might have
> done (1955, 36).

Chauncy apparently had done most of his reading prior to the Awakening in the writings of men who were supportive of orthodox views. Following the Awakening he spent seven years in an intense study of the Bible according to principles set forth by Arminian John Taylor of Norwich, who, among the English dissenters, was "the most influential and widely read in New England" (Wright 1955, 56-57, 76-78). Among other New Englanders influenced by Taylor, the most notable was Jonathan Mayhew, pastor of the West Church in Boston. Mayhew struck up a correspondence with the group of English dissenters associated with Taylor and, through their influence, obtained a Doctor of Divinity degree from Aberdeen (Wright 1955, 8, 79).

Taylor in his *Scripture-Doctrine of Original Sin* had set forth Arminian objections to the doctrine of the imputation of Adam's sin. He argued that guilt was a personal matter and that no one could be blamed for another's transgressions (Wright 1955, 84). Taking his cue from Taylor, and comparing Edwards's "identity of consciousness" concept (Edwards 1879, 1:222-27) to "Transubstantiation," Chauncy struck at the heart of Edwards's Calvinism. The starting point was the most vulnerable aspect of Edwards's doctrine--the damnation of infants on the basis of Adam's imputed sin (Wright 1955, 85-86; Haroutunian 1932, 134; Gerstner 1987, 43-44). Haroutunian noted that Chauncy did not publicly reject the whole Calvinistic system at once.

> As a Calvinist, knowing its connections with other less
> obnoxious doctrines, he was unwilling to commit himself to a

> denial of "eternal damnation," until 1782, when he published anonymously a pamphlet entitled *Salvation for All Men* (1932, 134).

Conrad Wright traced the step-by-step Arminian concession on the part of Chauncy and others.

> When the Arminians denied the doctrine of election, they said that God could never behave in so cruel and arbitrary a manner. When they denied original sin, they argued that a benevolent deity would not damn innocent infants. When they asserted that man is a free moral agent, they said that God would not create a being which lacked the power to do what was required of it. When they made regeneration a doctrine of development, they insisted that God's holy spirit is always striving with men for their salvation. In short, throughout their discussion of Christian doctrine, the Arminians were gradually reshaping the concept of the nature of God. They had become profoundly convinced that God is a benevolent deity, whose first concern is the happiness of his creatures (1955, 161).

For the Arminians, righteousness, or morality, was a matter of development through education and training, rather than spiritual regeneration. They believed that it was vastly more to God's credit to build the kingdom by appealing to moral men on the basis of ethical teaching than to expect an "immediate and violent act of the Holy Spirit." Man's salvation was regarded as within his own control in that God had decreed that men should be justified through their earnest efforts of obedience. Wright noted that the Arminian phase of men like Chauncy and Mayhew was particularly significant "because it retained the traditional vocabulary of Christian theology."

> It spoke of justification by faith, regeneration, sanctification, and perseverance at the same time that it had rebuilt the structure of which those doctrines had been part. In terms of theological development, . . . the point at which Arminianism became Unitarianism was where the old vocabulary disappeared, and the Arminian-Unitarian pattern clothed itself in new language (Wright 1955, 133-34).

As they moved progressively toward Unitarianism, Chauncy and Mayhew and their Arminian followers began to delve into the writings of the British moral philosophers--Locke, Shaftesbury, Hutcheson, Butler, and Hume (Wright 1955, 138-44).

> The Arminians found in Hutcheson an assertion of the natural capacity of all men for holiness; it is, said Chauncy, "common to all; as being a power the whole human race came into the world endowed with" (Wright 1955, 145).

Mayhew, like Chauncy, was obviously influenced by the benevolist doctrine of "moral sense." Conrad Wright cited the following passage from Mayhew's *Seven Sermons*:

> "Our Creator, besides endowing us with reason to distinguish betwixt moral good and evil, has moreover given us another faculty, which is sometimes called a *moral sense*. . . . By virtue of this faculty, moral good and evil, when they are objects to our minds, affect us in a very different manner; the first affording us pleasure, the other pain and uneasiness: And this, as unavoidably as the eye is differently affected with regular and irregular figures in the body; or the ear, with the most grateful harmony, and the most *harsh* and grating discord. . . ." (Wright 1955, 144).

In 1763 Mayhew published two Thanksgiving sermons on the *Nature, Extent, and Perfection of the Divine Goodness*, in which he "exalted God's benevolence above his wisdom and justice."

> If any man believes in reprobation, Mayhew said, his views cannot be reconciled with the goodness of God, for it is "most false and unscriptural, horrible to the last degree, to all men of an undepraved judgment, and blasphemous against the God of heaven and earth" (Wright 1955, 162).

Ironically, in his vehement denial of reprobation, he was confessing the doctrine of depravity--at least as it applied to the spiritual judgment of the Calvinists!

Wright stated that "the only extended analysis of the God of the Arminians was Chauncy's *Benevolence of the Deity*."

> This little volume was remarkable for the way in which it mirrored all the most popular eighteenth-century concepts: The sensational psychology, benevolence, optimism, the great chain of being, the theories of the British moralists, and

religious liberalism. It would be hard to find in New England a more complete surrender to the Age of Reason. It was one of those books which Chauncy wrote in the 1750's, but did not publish for over twenty years (Wright 1955, 163).

The position espoused by Charles Chauncy in *Benevolence of the Deity* could accurately have been described at once as rationalist, Arminian, benevolist, utilitarian, and moralistic.

Chauncy's benevolist concept of Deity was evident from the outset. In the introduction he stated,

> *A more shocking idea can scarce be given of the* Deity, *than that which represents him* as arbitrarily dooming the greater part of the race of men to eternal misery. *Was he wholly destitute of goodness, yea, positively* malevolent *in his nature, a worse representation could not be well made of him* (1784, viii).

Chauncy defined "Divine Benevolence" as a "*moral* attribute" and stated more particularly, "'A principle disposing and prompting to the communication of happiness' is the first idea that enters into its composition." Beings "endowed with perception" were the "proper objects of goodness: And goodness consists in a disposition to make them happy" (1784, 11).

The Arminian nature of Chauncy's concept of benevolence may be seen in its emphasis on freedom of choice. In fact there could be no virtue if there were no freedom of choice.

> Communicated happiness must be the *chosen act* of some *agent*, otherwise we never consider it as a *moral quality*, and call it *commendable* goodness. Accordingly, the *good man*, is not a mere *passive instrument* in the bestowment of good. . . . But he is a *good man* and he only, who *voluntarily* acts for the benefit of others. His offices of kindness are the result of *free choice*; and for this reason we apply goodness to him, under the notion of a *moral virtue* (Chauncy 1784, 12).

Chauncy's rationalism was carried forward into his concept of benevolence distinguishing it from the more voluntaristic benevolism of the Hutcheson school.

> In fine, "this disposition must be exercised under the guidance of *reason*, and in consistency with *right* and *fit conduct*": Nor otherwise do we consider it as a moral perfection (1784, 13).

The Cartesian emphasis on observation of human nature which had characterized seventeenth-century moral philosophy, was evident in Chauncy's benevolence doctrine.

> If we look within, and reflect upon our perceptions, we shall find, that our idea of benevolence, as a *commendable* quality, is not a *single* disposition; but a disposition exercised under the conduct of *intelligence*, and within the *limits* of *moral truth* and right (1784, 13).

For Chauncy, as had been the case for Hutcheson, metaphysics was predicated on observation of human nature.

> We can judge of the *benevolence* of the *Deity*, only from the ideas we have of benevolence in ourselves; removing away all the weaknesses, and adding infinite degrees of perfection (1784, 28).

Chauncy, of course, denied ourightly the doctrine of human depravity insisting instead, that just as a disposition of benevolence was inherent in the divine mind, so was it "with respect to ourselves."

> Benevolence is a disposition planted in our nature, and exists necessarily there. What I mean is we possess this turn of mind, disposition, or inclination, independently of our *own* choice; and yet, our exertions, in acts of beneficence, spring from *our wills*, which are determined *freely*, and not impelled by force (1874, 29).

Chauncy's concept of divine benevolence represented an Arminian attack on the Calvinistic doctrine of divine sovereignty, which had been so central to Edwards's perception of the beatific at his conversion (Edwards 1879, vol. 1, pp. liv-lv).

> Some there are, who, though they call the Deity benevolent, yet represent him as making some of his creatures and bestowing upon them riches of goodness with an express design, that they should misuse them, and by this means, give

occasion for the infliction of his wrath upon them, and in an enhanced measure, and this forever. Yea, there are those who make the infinitely benevolent God the *grand and only efficient*, not only in the bestowment of good, but even in the abuse of it . . . that its final result should be the everlasting damnation of a great number of the creatures his hands have formed. . . . What their idea of benevolence is I do not pretend to say. . . . And to attribute such malevolence to the all-perfect Deity is to make him, not constructively and by distant consequence, but directly and in explicit terms, a more malevolent being than even the evil one has ever been represented to be (Chauncy 1784, 31-32).

Edwards in *Original Sin* had previously responded to the very objection which Chauncy was raising, viz., that his doctrine made God directly responsible for human depravity.

In order to account for a sinful corruption of nature, yea a total native depravity of the heart of man, there is not the least need of supposing any evil quality, *infused*, *implanted*, or *wrought* into the nature of man, by any *positive* cause, or influence whatsoever, either from God, or the creature; or of supposing, that man is conceived and born with a *fountain of evil* in his heart, such as is anything properly *positive*. I think, a little attention to the nature of things will be sufficient to satisfy any impartial considerate inquirer, that the absence of good principles, and so the withholding of a special divine influence to impart and maintain those good principles--leaving the common natural principles of self-love, natural appetite, &c. to themselves, without the government of superior divine principles--will certainly be followed with the corruption; yea, the total corruption of the heart, without occasion for any *positive* influence at all: and that it was thus in fact that corruption in nature came on Adam, immediately on his fall, and comes on all his posterity, as sinning in him and falling with him (Edwards 1879, 1:217).

Edwards had insisted in *Freedom of the Will* that the divine decrees did *not* make God the Author of sin in the sense of "Agent" or "Actor."

But if, by *the Author of Sin*, is meant the permitter, or *not a hinderer* of Sin; and, at the same time, a disposer of the state of events, in such a manner, for wise, holy, and most excellent ends and purposes, that Sin, if it be permitted or not hindered, will most certainly and infallibly follow: I say, if

> this be all that is meant, by being the Author of Sin, I do not deny that God is the Author of Sin, (though I dislike and reject the phrase, as that which by use and custom is apt to carry another sense,) it is no reproach for the Most High to be thus the Author of Sin. This is not to be the *Actor of Sin*, but, on the contrary, *of holiness*. What God doth herein, is holy; and a glorious exercise of his nature (1879, 1:76).

> So inasmuch as sin is not the fruit of any positive agency or influence of the Most High, but, on the contrary, arises from the withholding of his action and energy, and, under certain circumstances, necessarily follows on the want of his influence; this is no argument that he is sinful, or his operation evil, or has any thing of the nature of evil. . . . It would be strange arguing, indeed, because men never commit sin, but only when God leaves them to *themselves*, and necessarily sin when he does, that therefore their sin is not *from themselves*, but from God; and so, that God must be a sinful being: as strange as it would be to argue, because it is always dark when the sun is gone, and never dark when the sun is present, that therefore all darkness is from the sun, and that his disk and beams must needs be black (1879, 1:77).

Chauncy could not conceive of the permission of sin as being consistent with God's benevolence. The snare which bedeviled Chauncy was that the "end" of his system was not the glory of God as it was for Edwards. For Edwards, man was morally obligated to shape his thoughts and actions to correspond to *God's Chief End*. For Chauncy, the definition of Deity had to be shaped to correspond to the mere humanitarian impulses of the social order.

> The making of a number of creatures with *malevolent affection* . . . is a method of conduct *unfit* in itself to promote the *common happiness*: Nor could it be constituted a *fit* method to attain this end, by any *will whatsoever*, not the will of the Supreme Sovereign himself. For *wrath*, *malice*, and *hatred*, are, in their natures, absolutely *unfit* to promote *social good* (Chauncy 1784, 34-35).

Chauncy, like Hutcheson, had become a social utilitarian. God's nature had to conform to men's social goals. Human happiness had become for Chauncy the measure of all things.

Just as a government was about to be overthrown because it failed to allow for the pursuit of the common happiness, so a system of theology that exalted God's sovereignty over man's freedom would be discarded. It was no mere coincidence that Jonathan Mayhew and Samuel Adams were to become intimate friends (Haroutunian 1932, 12). Samuel T. Logan, in his 1986 inaugural address as Professor of Church History at Westminster Seminary, spoke of the new "societal consensus" that rapidly developed in New England during the last half of the eighteenth century. The call for "rights" and "freedom" displaced the call for holiness that had once characterized the Puritan state. The new mood had been anticipated by John Wise, pastor of Ipswich, who as early as 1687 had led a raging protest against crown-appointed Governor Andros's tax levy. Perry Miller wrote of Joseph Dudley who tried Wise,

> What he had done, in short, was to give to his fellow Americans an entirely new sense of the value of the rights of Englishmen; in a flash he set these privileges (which to the founders were incidental to the pursuit of holiness, no more than instruments for obtaining it) in a wholly secular light, as matters pertaining to prescriptive right, grant, and precedent--entirely political in character, and to be maintained not out of Scripture but out of law, or else by stratagem ([1953] 1983, 156-57).

Logan cited two works written in 1757 as reflective of what had become the new colonial mood: Samuel Niles's *True Doctrine of Original Sin*, and Samuel Webster's *Winter Evening's Conversation upon the Doctrine of Original Sin*. Both authors affirmed that it was "unfair" to regard a man guilty for what Adam had done. Not even *God* had the right to charge a man with sins committed before his birth! This, said Logan, was the "theological equivalent of 'no taxation without representation'" (Logan 1986).

If Chauncy's doctrine of benevolence was utilitarian in the sense of being rooted in the value system of the emerging secular order, it must also be noted that the benevolence doctrine he propagated was *moralistic* rather than *pietistic*. Unlike Edwards who had defined true virtue as holiness consisting essentially in loving God supremely, Chauncy insisted that man could only be happy

> by an imitation of God in benignity of temper in conduct, in purity, in righteousness, in charity, and in every thing that is

amiable, and worthy of esteem. In this way God is happy; and in this way we may be happy also: but in no other (1784, 50).

Joseph Haroutunian in *Piety versus Moralism* described the subtle but marked shift in the social conscience as utilitarian values overtook Puritan New England,

> The new society's conscience dictated its own commands. Prosperous merchants have to be thrifty, industrious, dogged, sober, dependable, and decently selfish. They have to recognize their own responsibility for their success and failures, their own powers to earn and to control wealth, their innate endowments waiting for use and expansion. They have to realize that other men are similarly, perchance identically, constituted, wherefore they have a right to exercise their own powers and virtues, for their own success and prosperity. They have to respect others, to treat them as persons, or as ends unto themselves. In a word they must be *moral* (1932, xvi).

The liberal definition of "modern religion," according to Haroutunian, was nothing less than "modern secular morality."

> That God is the "moral Governor" of the world, that the relationship between God and man should be of the nature of "personal relationship," that God has given man a "free-will," and thus made him a "moral agent," thereby restricting His private power; that He purposes nothing that is not conducive to the happiness of man; that men have an innate capacity for good, that they have infinite possibilities for moral perfection, that they can and must cooperate with God to bring about the actualization of God's intended "moral kingdom"; that Jesus made human salvation possible through His revelation of the good life, that men ought to try to imitate Him; that sin consists in moral delinquency, and salvation, in the progressive achievement of a good life and the building up of moral personality, which is to be followed by the reward of the blessings of heaven, the abode of all good men;--the spirit of such religion is the spirit of modern morality, and not less secular for being a theory of things ultimate (1932, xvi-xvii).

Jonathan Edwards had unmasked such a deceitful image of religion in *The Nature of True Virtue*.

> The larger the number is, to which that private affection extends, the more apt men are, through the narrowness of their sight, to mistake it for true virtue; because then the private system appears to have more of the image of the universal. . . .
>
> And though self-love is far from being useless in the world, yea, it is exceeding necessary to society; yet every body sees that if it be not *subordinate* to, and regulated by, another more extensive principle, it may make a man a common *enemy* to the general system. And this is as true of *any other private affection*, notwithstanding its extent may be to a system that contains millions of individuals (1879, 1:137-38).

"Consistent Calvinism"

Charles Chauncy and company had stood on one side of the Great Awakening divide rejecting the revival in its entirety as "enthusiasm." On the other side, endorsing the Awakening as a whole, while recognizing the admixture of elements of "enthusiasm," was the group of men sympathetic to Edwards's theology and piety; most notably, Samuel Hopkins, Joseph Bellamy, Samuel Buell, Nathanael Emmons, and Jonathan Edwards, Jr. These men who regarded themselves as "Consistent Calvinists," and who later became known as the New Divinity school, were committed to perpetuating the theological legacy of their mentor. Joseph A. Conforti wrote of their profound influence,

> Between the Great Awakening and the establishment of the Yale Divinity School in 1882, theological education in Connecticut was largely in the hands of New Lights--especially New Divinity men (1981, 35).

Despite their profound influence, the New Divinity men encountered much opposition and ridicule in the socially elite circles of New England--particularly in the highly populated urban areas. Liberal Calvinist William Bentley of Salem derogatorily referred to them as "'Farmer Metaphysicians'." Indeed Bellamy had turned down a less than unanimous call to a church in New York City because he perceived that his social shortcomings were the basis for his less than full acceptance. Demographic studies have revealed that, in general, New Light ministers tended to come from the smaller hamlets and towns of

New England whereas the majority of Old Lights were natives of larger towns and cities (Conforti 1981, 9-15).

More significant than the relatively more modest background of the New Lights, was the nature of their teaching. They were commonly called "Hopkinsians," or "Hopkintonians," because of the prominent role held by Samuel Hopkins in preserving the Edwardsean theological legacy. Edwards, on his way to assume the presidency of the College of New Jersey in 1758, had placed a large collection of manuscripts in Hopkins's hands giving him permission to do with them as he saw fit. Following Edwards's death, his wife, Sarah, entrusted all of his manuscripts and library to Hopkins's care (Wright 1955, 115-16; Conforti 1981, 72). Hopkins pastored the church at Great Barrington from 1743 to 1769 and the First Congregational Church at Newport, Rhode Island from 1770 until his death in 1803. Conrad Wright singled out three earmarks of Hopkins's doctrinal system: (1) disinterested benevolence distinguished by a willingness to be damned for the glory of God (Conforti 1981, 120); (2) a depreciation of the use of means in the matter of salvation to the degree that the use of such means in a continued state of unrepentance rendered a man worthy of greater condemnation than if he had omitted their use; and (3) the idea that sin exists by God's design (Wright 1955, 116).

With respect to the first point it was noted in chapter 3 that Edwards had eschewed the concept of "a willingness to be damned for the glory of God" on the grounds that God did not require it. Edwards also considered such a doctrine to be inconsistent with the *enjoyment* of God which was inseparably connected to the *glorifying* of God. Hopkins in *True Holiness* denied the validity which Edwards in *True Virtue* had given to "self-love" as secondary beauty. Hopkins's formalization of the "willingness to be damned" doctrine in *A Dialogue between a Calvinist and a Semi-Calvinist* was published posthumously in 1805. Conforti paraphrased Hopkins's thesis of "disinterested benevolence" in this way: "In other words, one could not avoid damnation except by being willing to be damned" (1981, 120).

Hopkins's doctrine of disinterested benevolence took another non-Edwardsean twist. Whereas Edwards had located the epicenter of disinterested benevolence or true virtue in God's self-love, or the mutual love that subsists among the members of the Triune God, Hopkins in

The Nature of True Holiness insisted that benevolence must be "disinterested" in God, as well as man. Therefore God's benevolence was defined in terms of his inclination to make men happy totally apart from any motive of self-interest on God's part. In his *Sin . . . an advantage to the Universe*, Hopkins tried to have it both ways, affirming at once that God's holiness consisted in love to himself, as well as to the creature (Conforti 1981, 117-18). Thus it became apparent that the "Consistent Calvinists" were not as consistent as they might have imagined themselves.

Conforti stated that, whereas Edwards viewed virtue as a kind of "exalted consciousness," Hopkins defined it in terms of "elevated social behavior." "Consequently, evangelical activism superceded mystical quietism." In support of this observation, Conforti noted that Hopkins defined "Being in general" as a "tangible reality"--God and neighbor, rather than as a "comprehensive ontological reality" (1981, 117). While this distinction may be reflective of a difference in which the Gospel calling was lived out respectively by each man, Conforti's statement was somewhat misleading and misrepresentative of Edwards.

There was indeed a very practical side to Edwards's theology and the metaphysical expression "being in general" must be understood in the total context of Edwards's writing. Edwards spelled out the importance of the practical application of benevolence to the creatures, or love of neighbors, in *Religious Affections*. Part 3, section 12, was entitled, *"Gracious and holy affections have their exercise and fruit in Christian practice"* (1879, 1:314). Edwards went on to say that "Christian practice" was "*the chief* of all the signs of grace, both as an evidence of the sincerity of professors UNTO OTHERS, and also to their OWN CONSCIENCES" (1879, 1:320). Sections 13 and 14 continued this theme of "Christian practice" (1879, 1:321-36). In his discourse on *Justification by Faith* Edwards stressed the inseparable connection between justification and evangelical acts of obedience describing "works," according to the Letter of James, as being necessary and "manifestive" of justification (1879, 1:640-42, 649-52). Therefore, to categorize Edwards's theology as "mystical quietism," as Conforti did, was to misrepresent Edwards. There existed a theological base in Edwards's writings that was more than adequate to justify the kind of activistic social reform that was to characterize Hopkins's ministry at

Newport (Conforti 1981, 125-58). Thus, it was not necessary to compromise *the "highest end"* of the system as Hopkins did.

As for his depreciation of the means of grace, Hopkins's *Inquiry into the Promises of the Gospel* (1765) was a response to Jonathan Mayhew's *Striving to enter in at the strait gate, . . . And the Connexion of Salvation therewith, proved from the Holy Scriptures* published four years earlier. Mayhew had "stressed the spiritual efficacy of the means of grace and thus portrayed salvation as a conditional agreement" (Conforti 1981, 67, 69). Seeking to underline the unconditional nature of God's saving grace, Hopkins insisted that a sinner awakened through the means of grace was more despicable in the eyes of God, if he remained unregenerate, than an unawakened sinner who neglected the means. To many New England Congregationalists, it appeared that Hopkins had hamstrung himself. The Savoy Declaration, while insisting that works had no efficacy toward the salvation of unregenerate men, had nevertheless affirmed that "their neglect of them is more sinful and displeasing unto God" (Walker [1893] 1960, 384; Conforti 1981, 70). Hopkins's provocative statement seemed to destroy all conditional aspects of the covenant of grace and prompted Jedidiah Mills to suggest that the Hopkinsians were espousing a "strange" and "new" divinity. Mills's label stuck, and from the publication of his *Inquiry into the State of the Unregenerate under the Gospel* in 1767, Hopkinsians became the "New Divinity" school (Conforti 1981, 71).

Samuel Webster's *Winter-Evening's Conversation* had represented an attack on the doctrine of the imputation of Adam's sin by insisting that the doctrine made God the author of sin. In 1758 Bellamy responded to Webster in the *Wisdom of God in the Permission of Sin* following Edwards's lead by maintaining that God permitted sin simply by not hindering the expression of it. Hopkins, however, was not satisfied with Bellamy's response, and he carried the matter a step further in his *Sin . . . an Advantage to the Universe.* Hopkins stressed that God *willed* sin for "the sake of the great Good" that would result for the universe. Though sin was evil in nature, through the overruling sovereignty of God, its "consequences" were good (Conforti 1981, 66-67). Haroutunian stated that both Bellamy and Hopkins went beyond Edwards in their rationales for the existence of sin. Bellamy responded to the mood of the new social order and justified sin on the basis of human happiness--thus justifying God's government to eighteenth-century society. Hopkins, in Haroutunian's view, made the universe the "ultimate end," contrary to Edwards, for he justified the existence of sin on the basis that it was "an advantage to the universe" (Haroutunian 1932, 34, 39-40). Haroutunian also noted Hopkins's "hidden timidity" in avoiding the word "decree" in reference to God's will because of the unpopularity of the term (1932, 41). He cited Hopkins's definition of holiness--love to God, neighbor, and self--as a concession to the revolutionary era (1932, 84).

Haroutunian viewed Hopkins as one who "marks the transition from Calvinism to moralism."

> He was the astute apologist of Calvinistic theology; therefore his dialectical victories were achieved through the surrender of that which he set himself to defend (1932, 92).

Concerning Hopkins's sermon *On the Necessity of the Knowledge of God's Law in order to the Knowledge of Sin*, Haroutunian said,

> The aim of Hopkins' sermon is to show that sinners must know the perfect law of God which condemns them; that they must recognize their obligation to love it, though naturally they cannot but hate it (1932, 92).

Haroutunian sardonically summed up the deficiency of the New Divinity movement in the following statement:

> The profound tragedy of Edwards' theology was transformed into a farce by his would-be disciples, who used his language but ignored his piety (1932, 96).

Joseph Bellamy was the first of the New Divinity to appropriate Grotius's theory of the atonement. This "governmental" view of the atonement regarded the death of Christ as a public display of divine justice rather than a vicarious satisfaction. That such a view should become the official view of nineteenth-century Calvinist theologians--though not commonly accepted by grass roots evangelicals-- was reflective of the radical transformation in political thinking that prized "justice" much more than "sovereignty." In a revolutionary context, the governmental view of atonement meant that "Christ safe-guarded public good by displaying divine justice and moral government" (Haroutunian 1932, 171, 160-74). Haroutunian claimed that the New Divinity's espousal of governmental atonement which identified the Gospel with justice, instead of love, prompted further reaction on the part of the liberals against the Edwardseans. If there was indeed such a reaction to the governmental view of atonement as promulgated by Bellamy, and the other New Divinity men who followed his lead in the matter, it could not have been as great as the reaction against Edwards which their doctrine represented. In adopting Grotius's theory, the New Divinity school broadened considerably the Calvinistic doctrine claiming optimistically that the majority of the human race would probably be saved in view of projected population growth and millennial expectations (Conforti 1981, 165-66; Gerstner 1987, 102).

The reaction of the New England liberals was not only directed against the theology of the Edwardseans, broadening though it was, but ironically against an extreme form of liberalism. When an English preacher, John Murray, arrived in New England in the early 1770s and began proclaiming universal redemption through Christ, Chauncy and other Arminians shrewdly denounced such views and proceeded to set forth their own version of universal salvation. In 1782 Chauncy and John Clarke (also of Boston's First Church) published their *Salvation for All Men* in which they stated that eternal damnation was inconsistent with God's benevolence and that hell was disciplinary or reformatory rather than punitive (Conforti 1981, 164-65). Jonathan Edwards, Jr., responded most poignantly by stating that such a position destroyed the meaning of forgiveness. Forgiveness was exemption from a *"deserved penalty"* or *"penal evil."* According to Chauncy's and Clarke's definition of hell, therefore, forgiveness would represent the deprivation of a benefit, and thus the loss of happiness (Haroutunian 1932, 150). Haroutunian pointed out, however, that despite the dexterity of the argument, Jonathan Edwards, Jr., made it central to his argument that moral evil was punishable because it infringed upon "'the happiness of the universe'" (Haroutunian 1932, 151).

To summarize the role of the New Divinity, one must regard the movement as an attempt to defend the doctrine of divine sovereignty set forth in detailed precision by its mentor, Jonathan Edwards.

Unfortunately, Hopkins's doctrine of disinterested benevolence with its "willingness to be damned for the glory of God" emphasis, his depreciation of the means of grace, and his going beyond Edwards with respect to the will of God in the permission of sin, gave credence to Harriet Beecher Stowe's comparison of Consistent Calvinism "'to a rungless ladder with piety at the top'" (Berk 1971, 63). So much of the New Divinity rationale for Calvinism inadvertently made the good or happiness of the universe the ultimate end. This represented a concession to the benevolists from whose errors Edwards had sought to preserve the historic Christian doctrines.

Benevolist Arminian Evangelicalism

There were many parallels between Jonathan Edwards and his grandson, Timothy Dwight. Both were precocious in their childhood and youth. Both enrolled at Yale at the age of thirteen, graduated with valedictorian honors, earned masters degrees at Yale, and served as tutors at Yale. Both were ordained to the Christian ministry and achieved great reputation as preachers. Both attempted to lead their respective congregations away from the Half-Way Covenant--Edwards unsuccessfully, Dwight successfully. Both became college presidents. The most outstanding parallel was that both were key figures in spiritual awakenings (Winslow [1940] 1979; Cunningham 1942). Just as Jonathan Edwards had been the central human catalyst igniting the early New England revival fires to set the stage for the First Great Awakening, so Timothy Dwight became the human instrument used by God in initiating the Second Great Awakening among the student body at Yale. As the First Great Awakening had reached its peak in the evangelistic fervor of George Whitefield, so the Second Awakening would be extended through the ministries of Lyman Beecher and Nathaniel Taylor and reach its zenith in the ministry of one Charles Finney (Tyner 1977, 137-255; Cunningham 1942, 293-334; Hardman 1983, 109-28).

At Yale Dwight was facing full-fledged Infidelity in the forms of Deism, Unitarianism, and Atheism. The skepticism of Thomas Paine and others had greatly impacted the new republic during its revolutionary period (Cunningham 1942, 158-62). When Dwight began his duties as president of Yale in 1795, only two students were listed as members of the college chapel. Dwight met with the students to prepare for the annual forensic disputation. The students requested that the debate topic focus on the question: "Are the Scriptures of the Old and New Testaments the Word of God?" Former president Ezra Stiles had never permitted debate on that issue. Dwight chose a different approach. Refusing to dodge the issue, he encouraged the students to take their desired stand in opposition to the question while he himself took the pro side. The result was a gradual but steady conquest of Infidelity, a series of revivals, and a four-year cycle of lectures which Dwight developed and continued to deliver to the students over the span of his tenure. Most of Dwight's lecture material was contained in his systematic theology entitled *Theology Explained and Defended* (Cunningham 1942, 300-327).

Dwight's theology signalled the new trend in evangelism. In many ways Dwight represented the transition between revival as the "*Surprising Work of God*," as Edwards had described it, and the Charles G. Finney style of revival, according to which a revival was no more a miracle than a harvest of corn provided God's laws and appointed means be followed (Berk 1971, 161-99; Finney 1878, 4-7). Equally significant was the strange convergence of Arminianism and benevolism in the evangelical context of Dwight's ministry.

As Edwards had done, Timothy Dwight distinguished between God's "natural" and "moral" attributes. Among God's natural attributes were his unity, immutability, omnipresence, omniscience, omnipotence, and *independence*. Whereas Edwards had singled out "holiness" as the primary moral attribute of God, "holiness" was conspicuously absent from the list of attributes in Dwight's doctrine of God--although it did occur at other points in Dwight's lectures, most notably in his doctrine of Christ. Foremost among the divine attributes which Dwight enumerated was "Benevolence" (Edwards 1879, 1:279; Dwight 1863, 1:114-66; 2:153-93).

From the text, I John 4:8: "God is love," Dwight pointed out,

> It is not asserted that God is benevolent, but that he is Benevolence; or that Benevolence is the essence, the sum, of his being and character. . . . That Αγαπη signifies the kind of love, which in English is called Benevolence, will not, I presume be questioned (1863, 1:166).

The paramount importance which Dwight assigned to benevolence, or love, as the central attribute of God, may be seen from the following quotation from Dwight's *Theology*:

> In the Scriptures he has not required us to approve, admire, or love himself, in any character, except as a benevolent God (1863, 1:184).

How different was Dwight's focus from that of his grandfather!

> A true love to God must begin with a delight in his holiness, and not with a delight in any other attribute; for no other attribute is truly lovely without this, and no otherwise than as (according to our way of conceiving God) it derives its loveliness from this. Therefore, it is impossible that other attributes should appear lovely, in their true loveliness until this is seen: and it is impossible that any perfection of the divine nature should be loved with true love until this is loved. If the true *loveliness* of all God's perfections arises from the loveliness of his holiness; then the true love of all his perfections arises from the love of his holiness. They that do not see the glory of God's holiness, cannot see any thing of the true glory of his mercy and grace. They see nothing of the glory of those attributes, as any excellency of God's nature as it is in itself; though they be affected with them, and love them, as they concern their interest (Edwards 1879, 1:279).

For Dwight, it was God's benevolence, rather than his holiness, which comprised "his whole moral character."

> The whole moral character of God is love, endlessly diversified in its operations and manifestations, but simple and diversified in its nature, an intense and eternal flame of uncompounded good will (1863, 188-89).

Not only did Dwight affirm that "God is love," but the converse, as well: "Infinite Love is Infinite God" (1863, 1:186).

Dwight, like Chauncy, could speak of God in Shaftesbury-Hutchesonian terms.

> It is the essence of benevolence to love, and to produce happiness; and of infinite benevolence to love and to produce, infinite happiness. As, therefore, benevolence is the moving principle of the divine Mind, whence all its operations spring,

> and to which they are all conformed; it is evident, that with knowledge sufficient to contrive, and power sufficient to execute whatever it dictates, co-existing in the same Mind, all its dictates will be accomplished. The good, therefore, in which infinite benevolence delights, was originally chosen, has already begun, and is uninterruptedly pursued, and will be absolutely completed (1863, 1:384).

Human happiness was God's end in the design of the universe according to Dwight.

> That God made the universe with an intention to make it happy, and upon the whole, to make it supremely happy, will be denied by gross Infidels only (1863, 2:473).

> Benevolence is the love of happiness and the desire of its existence wherever it does not already exist (1863, 1:187).

Edwards had stated that "part of God's fulness" which he desired to communicate to his creatures was his "*happiness.*" This happiness, however, was God's joy and delight in his own Being (Edwards 1879, 1:101). The delight which God took in the creature's happiness was really a reflection of his own happiness communicated to the creature and reflected back to God. Thus, God's primary delight properly consisted in his own happiness (1879, 1:102). Edwards's focus was clearly God's delight in his own glory.

In Hopkinsian fashion, Dwight did what Edwards could never have done--he applied the doctrine of "disinterestedness" to the Being of God (Edwards 1879, 1:98). "God . . . is infinitely benevolent, and wholly disinterested" (1863, 2:474). Dwight's concept of divine benevolence, however, was not only "disinterested," it was manifestly utilitarian in that God's Being could only be validated as his benevolence was put to use for the benefit of the universe.

> It is not true that God would be or would ever have been, thus perfectly happy, had he not made the Universe; or were he not to conduct it for the purpose for which it was made. Benevolence like gold, finds its chief value in its use. *It is*, in the nature of the case, *more blessed to give than to receive*; or to be in any other employment or situation (1863, 1:186).

Edwards, of course, had never denied God's attribute of benevolence as being expressed in the creation of the world. For Edwards, however, God's benevolence to his creatures was secondary to, and yet implicit in, his highest end of seeking his own glory.

> Indeed, after the creatures are *intended* to be created, God may be conceived of as being moved by benevolence to them, in the strictest sense, in his dealings with them. His exercising his goodness to them and gratifying his benevolence to them in particular, may be the spring of all God's proceedings through the universe; as being now the determined way of gratifying his general inclination to diffuse himself. Here God acting for *himself*, or making himself his last end, and his acting for *their* sake, are not to be set in opposition; they are rather to be considered as coinciding one with the other. But yet God is to be considered as first and original in his regard; and the creature is the object of God's regard, consequently, and by implication, as being as it were comprehended in God (1879, 1:101).

For Dwight, on the other hand,

> The highest blessedness . . . and the greatest glory, is found in communicating good, and not in gaining it. . . . The great design of God in all things is, therefore to do good, boundlessly, and forever (1863, 1:85).

Dwight did tacitly acknowledge the "infinite complacency" that subsisted among the members of the Godhead (1863, 2:193), and he even observed the connection between that intra-Trinitarian love of complacence, and love of benevolence in the creature.

> That God delights with infinite complacency in his own moral character, cannot be questioned. Benevolence in his Intelligent creatures is a direct resemblance of this character; his own image, instamped on created minds; and cannot fail, therefore, to be an object of the same complacency, wherever it exists (1863, 1:190).

The difference between Dwight and Edwards was that Dwight, by making benevolence the object of complacence, fell into the circular reasoning trap which Edwards had avoided by making "BEING, simply considered" the "first object of a truly virtuous benevolence." Edwards had argued, "If virtue consises [consists] primarily in love to virtue, then virtue, the thing loved, is the love of virtue: so that virtue must consist in the love of the love of virtue--and so on in infinitum" (1879, 1:123). In Edwards's system, "being" came before "beauty," "existence" before "excellence." This priority of being was what underlay Edwards's "theological objectivism." Edwards did not espouse beauty for beauty's sake, or virtue for the sake of virtue. God, the "Being of beings" was the highest end in Edwards's theological scheme; and the intra-Trinitarian complacence was founded primarily on the basis of *being* and secondarily on the basis of virtuous *beauty*. Virtue was therefore defined in reference to God--"the foundation and fountain of all being and all beauty." His "Being" was the *primary* ground of love--that is to say, virtue consisted primarily in "LOVE TO GOD"--"infinitely the greatest Being"; and his "moral excellency" was the *secondary* ground of love (Edwards 1879, 1:125).

A further difference between Dwight and Edwards, in regard to the intra-Trinitarian love of complacency, was that Dwight, lacking Edwards's distinct doctrine of divine holiness, was unable to uphold God's glory as being infinitely worthy in itself, totally apart from any benevolence expressed toward the creature (Edwards 1879, 1:97-98, 274-81).

As a result of Dwight's failure to ground virtue in "being," as well as his neglect of divine holiness, Dwight's doctrine of the intra-Trinitarian love of complacency did not have the same impact upon his theological system as Edwards's doctrine had had upon his. Lacking the foundation, Dwight was unable to uphold that doctrine consistently, or to express it in terms of divine self-love as Edwards had done, and Augustine and Malebranche, before him.

The doctrine of divine benevolence which Dwight espoused and set before the students at Yale was the "disinterested" version. Dwight's primary focus was clearly on the creature's benefit in terms of happiness, whereas Edwards's had been on the Creator's gain in terms of glory. Dwight was the Christian utilitarian; Edwards, the Christian ontologician. Dwight was the Christian humanitarian describing the formula for human happiness; Edwards, the Christian theologian describing the beauty of holiness.

Edwards had not been concerned to protect God's reputation by assigning the term "disinterested" to the divine benevolence, as though God's self-love implied the vice of a selfish spirit as it was commonly regarded in the creature. In the first place, God's private interest could not be regarded as opposed to the public good since he was "the author and head of the whole system" (Edwards 1879, 1:103).

> But now, with respect to the Divine Being, there is no such thing as confined selfishness in him, or a love to himself *opposite* to general benevolence. It is impossible, because he comprehends all entity, and all excellence, in his own essence (Edwards 1879, 1:105).
>
> God in seeking his glory, seeks the good of his creatures; because the emanation of his glory (which he seeks and delights in, as he delights in himself and his own eternal glory) implies the communicated excellency and happiness of his creatures. And in communicating his fulness for them, he does it for himself; because their good, which he seeks, is so much in union and communion with himself. God is their good. Their excellency and happiness is nothing, but the emanation and expression of God's glory: God, in seeking their glory and happiness, seeks himself: and in seeking himself, *i.e.* himself diffused and expressed, (which he delights in, as he delights in his own beauty and fulness), he seeks their glory and happiness. . . .
> . . . "He that loveth his wife loveth himself--even as the Lord the church; for we are members of his body, of his flesh, and of his bones" (Edwards 1879, 1:105).

Second, to suggest that God had some evil ulterior motive in seeking his own happiness primarily, was an absurd notion implying that God was, or should have been, *dependent* on the creature for his own happiness.

> God making himself his end, argues no dependence; but is consistent with absolute independence and self-sufficiency (Edwards 1879, 1:105).
>
> Though he has real pleasure in the creature's holiness and happiness, yet this is not properly any pleasure which he receives from the creature. For these things are what he *gives* the creature. They are wholly and entirely from him. . . .

> From this view, it appears, that nothing has been said, in the least inconsistent with those expressions in Scripture, that signify, "man cannot be profitable to God," &c. For . . . God is absolutely independent of us. . . . We have nothing of our own, no stock from whence we can give to God; and . . . no part of his happiness originates from man (Edwards 1879, 1:102).

Dwight practically set forth his theological apologetic on the basis of human self-interest; thus, the Christian message was true because it was humanitarian and beneficial to the social order. His exposition of the divine attributes was explicitly utilitarian. God's justice was regarded as something in which "the world is infinitely interested" (1863, 1:195). God's truth was to be esteemed because "no society can exist without confidence; and no confidence without truth" (1863, 1:203). The eternity of God's Being became, for Dwight, a theological necessity in that it enabled God to execute his benevolent designs "in an everlasting progress and to complete for ever the Infinite good which he has begun" (1863, 1:133).

Dwight did, however, repudiate the Shaftesburian thesis that the virtue of disinterested benevolence in man could not co-exist with "any hope of reward, or any fear of punishment." Instead he distinguished between "disinterestedness" and "uninterestedness," the latter of which he regarded as absurd. *Our happiness is a desirable object*; and deserves to be sought in a certain degree." Disinterestedness was a "concern for happiness"; uninterestedness was "no concern for happiness" (Dwight 1863, 2:487-96). Clearly Dwight would never have acceded to the Hopkinsian "willingness to be damned" doctrine.

Dwight's criticism of Shaftesbury, however, belied the pervasion of his own theological system by elements of the Shaftesbury-Hutcheson gospel. In addition to his concession to benevolism, Dwight's theology represented a decided compromise with the very Arminianism which his grandfather had regarded as "*the* enemy in the New England of his day" (Bogue 1975, Note, 77). In particular, he was unable to affirm, as had Edwards, the five points of Dort. Though he believed in depravity, he came short of affirming *total* depravity (1863, 1:461). Calvin, of course, had not insisted that the image of God in man had been so ruined as to be obliterated; nor had Edwards defined *total depravity* in such an extreme way.

> Men of sound judgment will always be sure that a sense of divinity which can never be effaced is engraved upon men's minds (Calvin 1960, 1:45).

Dwight maintained that Adam's sin, but *not* his guilt, had been transferred to the entire race, thus rejecting the Edwardsean doctrine of imputation (Dwight 1863, 1:478). Dwight was concerned so as not to make God the "efficient cause of sin." As to the Hopkinsian thesis that sin was an "advantage to the Universe," Dwight would only subscribe in a negative way.

> It cannot be proved that the existence of sin will, in the end be a detriment to the Universe. . . . It can never be proved that the existence of moral evil is injurious to the Universe; or the permission of it, inconsistent with the most perfect good-will on the part of God. At the same time, I acknowledge myself unable, and my complete conviction, [is] that all other men are unable, to explain this subject so as to give an inquirer clear and satisfactory views, by the light of Reason, of the propriety of permitting the introduction of moral evil into the Intelligent system (1863, 1:175).

Wayne Tyner in *The Theology of Timothy Dwight in Historical Perspective* stated that

> Dwight's doctrine of man . . . reveals a weakening if not a total abandonment of the idea of man's moral inability (1977, 226-27).

Stephen Berk quoted Dwight as saying,

> "Perhaps no one who persisted in his efforts to gain eternal life was ever finally deserted by the Spirit of grace" (Berk 1971, 94).

In reference to this statement, which was an inversion of irresistible grace, as well as a denial of moral inability, Berk commented,

> This affirmation of unregenerate attempts to procure salvation was closer to Old Calvinism and Arminianism than to the New Divinity (1971, 95).

Inasmuch as Dwight's mentor had been Jonathan Edwards, Jr. (Cunningham 1942, 55), such a departure from the New Divinity emphasis on moral inability was remarkable, and, in view of Dwight's own lectures, contradictory. Dwight's lecture entitled "Man's Inability To Obey The Law of God" spoke of man's "*indisposition*" or "*disinclination to obedience*" that was "*so obstinate and enduring,*" that it was "*never relinquished by man, except when under the renewing influence of the Spirit of God.*" This "indisposition" Dwight distinguished from man's "natural powers" which "are plainly sufficient." "Our inclination only is defective" (Dwight 1863, 4:21). Whatever "weakening" Tyner and Berk observed in Dwight's regard for moral inability, it was obvious Dwight did not abandon the doctrine altogether; but his inconsistency in the matter was all too obvious and somewhat puzzling.

For Dwight, sin consisted in "a preference of ourselves to others, and to all others, to the universe and to God."

> That is sin, and all that in the Scripture is meant by sin (1863, 2:493).

In Dwight's view, the spiritual death resulting from Adam's sin

> cuts up by the roots, all inclination in rational beings to befriend each other; and prompts them to become, as much as possible, the means of each other's misery (1863, 1:427).

As Dwight reflected on man's chief end, happiness, and thought on man's sin, selfishness, he postulated the need of regeneration: "The native disposition of man, is opposed to the end of his being" (1863, 1:391).

Dwight's compromise on the second Dort issue, *unconditional election*, was evident in that he, like Samuel Hopkins, was not comfortable in speaking of God's "decrees." Dwight preferred the word "choice" or "pleasure" thus softening the doctrine of divine sovereignty (1863, 1:242).

> *God cannot but have chosen the existence of all those things, whose existence was on the whole desirable, and of no others.*

> ... The benevolence of the Divine character furnishes complete evidence of the Truth of this position (1863, 1:244).

Whereas Edwards had allowed for some points of similarity between his doctrine of "moral necessity" and the doctrine of the Stoic philosophers (1879, 1:69), Dwight rejected outrightly any point of comparison of Stoicism with his doctrine.

> I cannot perceive a similarity between an unintelligent and involuntary series of causes, compelling by natural necessity, or coercion, the existence of their consequent effects, and controlling by inevitable necessity the actions of both God and Men; and the free, wise and voluntary, agency of the infinitely intelligent and benevolent Mind, originally planning, and steadily executing, a system of infinite good, according to the dictates of his boundless wisdom, and perfect pleasure (1863, 1:252).

Dwight plainly rejected the third point of Dort in adopting the Hopkinsian view of *general* atonement which made salvation a "possibility" for all men rather than a reality for some.

> The first grand effect of the Redemption of Christ, is to render it possible for man to become holy, in order to his justification, and adoption (1863, 1:501).

Tyner commented (but not without revealing his own Arminianism),

> Pointing up one of the major weaknesses of Old Calvinism, Dwight noted that if the Atonement of Christ covered only the elect, then salvation is not really offered to other men. Therefore they cannot be guilty of rejecting Christ for his atonement did not apply to them.... While the way is open to all, no man is pardoned merely because of the atonement. He must accept the atonement by faith (Tyner 1977, 221-22).

Dwight's dissatisfaction with the Dort doctrine of irresistible grace was apparent in the following statement:

> When it is said, that the agency of the Divine Spirit in renewing the heart of man is *irresistible* it is probably said, because this agency being an exertion of omnipotence is concluded, of course to be irresistible by human power. This

> seems not, however, to be said on solid grounds. That agency of the Holy Ghost, which St. Stephens informs us was resisted by the Jews, and by their fathers, was an exertion of the same omnipotence, and was resisted by human power. I know of nothing in the regenerating agency of the same Spirit, except the fact, that it is never resisted, which proves it to be irresistible, any more than that which the Jews actually resisted. That the Spirit of God can do any thing with man, and constitute man any thing which he pleases cannot be questioned. But that he will exert a regenerating agency on the human mind which man has not a natural power to resist, or which man could not resist if he would is far from being satisfactory evident to me. Indeed, I am ready to question whether this very language does not lead the mind to views concerning this subject which are radically erroneous (Dwight 1863, 3:21-27; Tyner 1977, 236).

Dwight's choice of words, "man has not a natural power to resist," betrayed a misunderstanding, or ignorance, of the Edwardsean teaching on Dort's fourth point. Edwards had never questioned the *natural ability*, either of the elect or of the non-elect, to resist the regenerating grace of the Spirit of God. He certainly had not doubted the *moral ability* of the non-elect to resist the agency of the Spirit. Edwards did, however, insist on the *moral inability* of the *elect* to resist the regenerating agency of the Holy Spirit.

> We are said to be *naturally* unable to do a thing, when we cannot do it if we will, because what is most commonly called *nature* does not allow of it, or because of some impeding defect or obstacle that is extrinsic to the Will; either in the faculty of understanding, constitution of body, or external objects. *Moral* Inability consists not in any of these things; but either in the want of inclination; or the strength of a contrary inclination; or the want of sufficient motives in view, to induce and excite the act of the Will, or the strength of apparent motives to the contrary. Or both of these may be resolved into one; and it may be said in a word, that moral Inability consists in the opposition or want of inclination.

As an example of "*moral Inability*" Edwards stated,

> A woman of great honour and chastity may have a moral Inability to prostitute herself to her slave. . . . A strong habit of virtue, and a great degree of holiness, may cause a moral Inability to love wickedness in general, and may render a man

unable to take complacence in wicked persons or things; or to choose a wicked in preference to a virtuous life (1879, 1:11).

Describing the issue of regeneration in his *Treatise Concerning Religious Affections*, Edwards struck at the very heart of the matter of moral inability in regard to the doctrine of irresistible grace.

> Saints and angels behold the *beauty of God's holiness*: and this sight only, will melt and humble the hearts of men, wean them from the world, draw them to God, and effectually change them. A sight of the awful greatness of God may overpower men's *strength*, and be more than they can endure; but if the *moral* beauty of God be hid, the enmity of the *heart* will remain in its full strength. No love will be kindled, the will, instead of being effectually gained, will remain inflexible; whereas the first glimpse of the moral and spiritual glory of God shining into the heart, produces all these effects with a power which nothing can withstand (1879, 1:281).

In view of the above quotation from Edwards's *Religious Affections* it might fairly be asked whether Dwight's relative disregard for the doctrine of divine holiness contributed to his denial of the doctrine of irresistible grace.

Concerning Dort's fifth point, the perseverance of the saints, Dwight's position was certainly weakened by his view of regeneration whereby the state of the new believer was virtually the same as that of Adam prior to the Fall (Dwight 1863, 2:419; Tyner 234-35, 240). Edwards had repudiated such an Arminian conception in that it guaranteed the regenerate person nothing more than a new probationary state thus placing him once again under a covenant of works (1879, 1:636).

The new moralism which had become so characteristic of New England Arminianism in the revolutionary era was a dominant feature of Dwight's theological lecture series. Dwight viewed the Gospel in one sense as "Law," even entitling one of his lectures "Justification--The Duty of Believing" (1863, 1:451; 2:312-23). Dwight parted company with the New Divinity, and exceeded Old Calvinism, in viewing "'means' as instruments influencing men to accept Christ--a concept essential to all evangelism since Dwight's day" (Tyner 1977, 239). In volume 4 of Dwight's *Theology Explained and Defended*, no less than twenty-seven sermons were devoted to the means of grace. Tyner wrote,

> He stood at the threshold . . . where theology passed to an era in which revivals were "worked up" rather than "waited for" or "prayed down" and an era in which free moral agency triumphed over depravity (1977, 264).

The triumph of "free moral agency" over "depravity" was the triumph of Arminianism in New England.

Lyman Beecher and Nathaniel Taylor, Dwight's proteges, were to adopt revival techniques that Dwight himself would consider too liberal. They would press the individual for conversion; Dwight simply encouraged the individual to use the means of grace. Dwight gave his students an activist theology bridging the Hopkinsian gap between human means and God's grace. Thereby he opened the way for man to become the cause of his own choices (Berk 1971, 91; Tyner 1977, 249-54).

Dwight's compromise on some of Dort's five points, and his outright denial of the others, represented a definite break with the Calvinism Edwards had espoused. While his benevolent theology, unlike Chauncy's, did not consider the admission of Evil to be inconsistent with the "greatest possible Good" which God would bring about though "Redemption" (1863, 1:117), Dwight's doctrine of divine sovereignty was certainly obscured and superceded by his doctrine of benevolence. For a Calvinist, it was a long way from the theological objectivism of Edwards, that defined virtue as consisting chiefly in "a supreme love to God" who was the "sum and comprehension of all existence and excellence," to the benevolent world of Timothy Dwight (Edwards 1879, 1:125).

> Love to Man is the only source of voluntary beneficence to Man. The *Love, which is the fulfilling of the Law* is a vital and immortal principle of doing good to all men, both friends and enemies, at all times, and in every manner. Nor is there any real and voluntary beneficence, except which springs from this principle. Rational Beings, wholly under its influence, would form a perfect state of happiness in any world, and such beings, freed from all restraints, would, if destitute of it, create consummate misery. He, then, who refuses obedience to this Law, is guilty of gross injustice to God, relinquishes all personal excellence, peace, happiness, and worth: and

> renouncing all voluntary usefulness on the one hand, prepares himself, on the other, to become a nuisance to the Universe (Dwight 1863, 1:450-51).

In his *Genetic History of the New England Theology*, Frank Hugh Foster expressed the irony of Edwards's theological heirs:

> To agree with Edwards was still the high ambition of them all; and when they consciously disagreed . . . they thought they were only better expressing Edwards' true meaning (Foster [1907] 1987, 369).

CONCLUSION

Synopsis

For Jonathan Edwards the beatific was basic. To try to understand Edwards's life and works on any basis other than a dawning of the beatific with its biblical focus in divine sovereignty is a futile effort. Lockean empiricism was only a part of the late seventeenth- and early eighteenth-century moral philosophical landscape in which he moved and against which he set forth the historic doctrines of the Christian faith. Psychological empiricism was not the essence of Edwards's message, but rather the idiom of expression. Metaphysics never constituted the final substance of the message, but was frequently employed as the language of communication, and always with a theological purpose.

Though philosophy was useful to Edwards as a means of setting forth, synthesizing, and clarifying theological issues, it was subordinated to divine revelation. Ethics was not autonomous in Edwards's system but was inextricably related to ontology. Ontology in turn, was related to theology and was subject to it. Morality, in the pure sense, was founded only in regeneration. Love to God, rather than concern for the public welfare, was for Edwards the highest end of moral philosophy.

The aesthetic frame of Edwards's moral philosophy suggested that God could not be glorified without, at the same time, being enjoyed. Human happiness and self-love, however, were subordinate to, and reached their proper fulfillment in, God's happiness; and God's chief happiness was centered in his own holiness. Benevolence was rooted in the divine self-love, that mutual love subsisting among the members of the Triune God.

For Edwards, Calvinism, which glorified God by making man totally dependent on the sovereign God in the matter of salvation, was preferable to Arminianism, which reversed the order of dependence. The work of redemption was God's means to his end of communicating his own glorious fulness *ad extra*. The history of redemption was rooted in the intra-Trinitarian covenant in which each member of the Godhead sought the glory of the other. Redemption was historically implemented in terms of a covenant of grace. Creation was subordinated to redemption and the covenant of works to the covenant of grace in order that God's most glorious attributes might be magnified.

It is evident that all of Edwards's life and thought moved inexorably toward one grand final focus, the glory of God.

The Legacy of Edwards

Edwards's life and works stand as a prophetic challenge to the church. Each new generation of the church must become captivated by the beatific or cease to be the church by catering to the secular demands of society. Nothing short of a prayerful encounter with the living God through his Word and Spirit, submission to his sovereignty, and delight in his holiness is worthy of the name Christian.

Edwards's prophetic challenge to the church involves redeeming the secular idiom. The church must cast the Gospel message in thought forms distinctive to each new generation, and she must actively re-direct the lines of secular thought Godward. Christian thought and spirit must not be bifurcated resulting in an emphasis on one to the neglect of the other. The church's sons, illumined by the beatific and gifted in thinking skills, must extend the lines of biblical truth into the dark world of philosophy, and indeed into all branches of human learning. The Edwardsean legacy represents a call to re-establish theology as the queen of the sciences, not in terms of a rigidity that stifles scholarship or scientific inquiry, but rather in the form of a lucid and forceful assertion of the Holy Scriptures as the fountainhead of all human academic endeavor.

Neither systematic theology nor sound doctrine ought to be regarded as irrelevant or inimical to the revitalization of the church by the Holy Spirit. Indeed, they are essential for her purity, upbuilding, and peace. And if there is indeed a place for systematic theology in the contemporary church, as a means of establishing sound doctrine, then that system which most glorifies God, by making man most dependent upon God in the matter of salvation, ought to be taught in the seminaries and expounded from the pulpits. The doctrine of God's determinate foreknowledge and the eternal covenant of redemption ought not to be skirted, or regarded as too controversial for this generation; indeed, God's electing grace ought to be proclaimed as the very fabric of the Gospel.

Edwards's legacy demands that the unsanctified gods of self-love be renounced in the face of the ugly truth of total depravity with its insidious ongoing effects even among the sanctified in this present order. The employment of manipulative tactics stemming from man's natural craving for power and knowledge must give way to a ministry occupied with the beauty of holiness. Thus, the church never outgrows its need for repentance.

Edwards's unique theological contribution to the church, with its foundation in divine self-love and focus on God's glory as the chief end, will undoubtedly be the springboard for further study, theological reflection, and spiritual renewal. One particular area for further study, which Norman Fiering has uncovered, is the matter and degree of Edwards's theological indebtedness to the Frenchman Nicolas Malebranche (Fiering 1981a).

Finally, Edwards's legacy sounds a clarion call for one or more of Zion's sons to complete the *Summa* envisioned by the Puritan pastor-theologian. The summons to a *Summa*, a grand synthesis of secular and church history embracing "the whole body of divinity," moving climactically toward the final state of things, and issuing in the glory of God, represents the unfinished part of the Edwardsean legacy. This would indeed be a "Gargantuan undertaking" (Winslow [1940] 1979, 310). Perhaps no saint this side of glory could contain the illumination from the dawn of the beatific, from which such a work must surely proceed, even if he were endowed with the requisite intellectual gifts (Ps 131:1).

Thus, it is fit, since there is an infinite fountain of light and knowledge, that this light should shine forth in beams of communicated knowledge and understanding; and, as there is an infinite fountain of holiness, moral excellence, and beauty, that so it should flow out in communicated holiness. And that, as there is an infinite fulness of joy and happiness, so these should have an emanation, and become a fountain flowing out in abundant streams, as beams from the sun.

Thus it appears reasonable to suppose, that it was God's last end, that there might be a glorious and abundant emanation of good *ad extra*, or without [external to] himself; and that the disposition to communicate himself . . . was what moved him to create the world (Edwards 1879, 1:100).

APPENDIX

Edwards and the "Lapsarian" Issue

Edwards's magnifying the glory of Christ's redemption over and above the glory of a hypothetically unfallen Adam suggested supralapsarianism, especially in view of God's eternal covenantal design and his supreme end to manifest his glory to the highest degree (Edwards 1879, 1:187, 536). The supralapsarian scheme meant that the divine decree of redemption of an elect people involving a covenant of grace would have preceded the decree concerning creation and the Fall of man (Latourette 1953, 765).

Regarding the eternal "covenant of redemption," Edwards said,

> There were things done at the *creation* of the world, in order to that work; for the world itself seems to have been created in order to it (1879, 1:534).

The above quotation clearly made redemption the *end* (though not the supreme end) of creation in Edwards's theological system. On the basis of Edwards's first principle concerning the ordering of the decrees, such a statement was tantamount to supralapsarianism.

> When one thing decreed is the end of another, this must in some respect be conceived of as prior to that other (1879, 2:540).

Indeed such a position was consistent with Calvin:

> Surely, the fall of Adam is not presupposed as preceding God's decree in time; it is what God determined before all ages (Calvin 1960, 1:469).

To ascribe supralapsarianism to Edwards, on the above basis, however, was to underestimate his precisionism and to overlook his definitive statement on the lapsarian issue contained in *Miscellaneous Remarks: Concerning the Divine Decrees*.

For Edwards, some things pertaining to the Divine decrees of election and reprobation were indeed antecedent to the decree concerning creation and the Fall. Regarding the election decree, God's "design to communicate and glorify his goodness and love eternally to a certain number" was considered as prior to the decree of "man's being and fall." In regard to reprobation, God's general decree to glorify his own justice preceded the decree of the creation and Fall.

While some things related to these decrees did indeed precede the decree of the creation and Fall,

> yet both the decree of election and rejection or reprobation . . . must be considered as consequent on the decrees concerning the creation and fall. For both these decrees have respect to that distinction or discrimination that is afterwards actually made amongst men in the pursuance of these decrees. Hence effectual calling, being the proper execution of election, is sometimes in Scripture called election; and the rejection of men in time is called reprobation. . . .
>
> The decrees of God must be conceived of in the same order, and as antecedent to, and consequent on, one another, in the same manner, as God's acts in the execution of these decrees (Edwards 1879, 2:541).

Inasmuch as the election decree involved the glorifying of God's mercy and grace, man's sinfulness and unworthiness were presupposed (1879, 2:541). Inasmuch as the sinfulness of the reprobate was the "ground" or "foundation of both the fitness and possibility" of divine "justice being glorified in the punishment of sin," the decree of reprobation had to be subsequent to the creation and Fall of man.

> So both the sin of the reprobate and also the glory of divine justice, may properly be said to be before the decree of damning the reprobate (Edwards 1879, 2:540).

Unlike reprobation, election was decreed antecedently of any attending human acts.

> God in the decree of election is justly to be considered as decreeing the creature's eternal happiness, antecedently to any foresight of good works, in a sense wherein he does not in reprobation decree the creature's eternal misery, antecedently to any foresight of sin. . . . But faith and good works are not supposed in the first place in order to the decree of election. The first things in order in this decree are, that God will communicate his happiness, and glorify his grace (Edwards 1879, 2:540).

Edwards's doctrine of the decrees, thus, explicitly represented *infralapsarianism* as distinct from *supralapsarian* in that it regarded the decrees of election and reprobation as posterior to the decree of the creation and Fall of man (Latourette 1953, 765). Edwards, however, was careful to distinguish his infralapsarianism from Arminianism which made "God's determination" dependent on "the creature's sinful act, as an event, the coming to pass of which primarily depends on the creature's determination" (1879, 2:540). For Edwards, the Arminian position implied mutability in the Godhead and made

> the grand contrivance for our redemption, and destroying the works of the devil, by the Messiah, and all the great things God has done in the prosecution of these designs, . . . only the fruits of his own disappointment (1879, 1:34, 35).

Edwards avoided the heresy of divine mutability in that God's prior decree to manifest his own glory "to a certain select number" assured that redemption would be devised and accomplished, though *consequent* upon the Fall of man. Divine immutability was further safeguarded in Edwards's system in that the Fall itself was divinely decreed, though in a permissive sense, with "respect to the great good that he will make it an occasion of" (1879, 2:529).

The dilemma of Edwards's explicit infralapsarianism juxtaposed with an implicit supralapsarianism (with respect to redemption) may be accounted for on a twofold basis. First, Edwards himself acknowledged that the doctrine of the decrees was "mysterious" and "attended with difficulties," though "the opposite doctrine" of Arminianism was "more mysterious, and attended with greater difficulties" (1879, 2:543). Second, the lapsarian dilemma posed by Edwards's writings was epitomized by his understanding of the cross as embracing, at once, the decree of the ultimate expression of sin and the decree concerning the infinite glory of redemption. This may well hold the key to resolving the lapsarian issue in Edwards's system.

> The sin of crucifying Christ being foreordained of God in his decree, and ordered in his providence, of which we have abundant evidence from the nature of the thing, and from the great ends God had to accomplish by means of this wicked act of crucifying Christ; it being, as it were, the cause of all the decrees, the greatest of all decreed events, and that on which all other decreed events depend as their main foundation; being the main thing in the greatest work of God, the work of redemption, which is the end of all other works; and it being so much prophesied of, and so plainly spoken of, as being done according to the determinate counsel and foreknowledge of God; I say, seeing we have such evidence that this sin is foreordained in God's decrees, and ordered in providence, and it being, as it were, the head sin, and representative of the sin of men in general; hence is a clear argument, that all the sins of men are foreordained and ordered by a wise Providence (1879, 2:528).

Thus, on the basis of the "head sin" Edwards could predicate God's decree of the Fall in infralapsarian fashion as redemption presupposed it; and, in seeming contradiction, he could insist that redemption was the "end of all other works."

REFERENCE LIST

Ahlstrom, Sydney E. 1972. *A religious history of the American people.* New Haven: Yale University Press.

Alleine, Joseph. 1959. *An alarm to the unconverted.* Evansville: Sovereign Grace Publishers.

Ames, William. [1629] 1983. *The marrow of theology.* Translated from 3d Latin edition and edited by John D. Eusden. Durham, NC: Labyrinth Press.

Anderson, Wallace. 1980. Introduction to *The scientific and philosophical writings.* Vol. 6. *The works of Jonathan Edwards.* New Haven: Yale Press.

Augustine, St. 1958. *The city of God.* An abridged version from the translation by Gerald G. Walsh et al. Edited and introduced by Vernon J. Bourke. Garden City, NY: Doubleday & Co.

————. n.d. *The confessions of St. Augustine,* ed. E. B. Pusey. London: Thomas Nelson and Sons Ltd.

Avey, Albert E. [1954] 1961. *Handbook in the history of philosophy: A chronological history of western thought, 3500 B. C. to the present.* 2d edition. New York: Barnes & Noble, Inc.

Berk, Stephen E. 1971. *Calvinism versus democracy.* Hamden, CT: Archon Books.

Bettenson, Henry. [1943] 1963. *Documents of the Christian church.* 2d edition. London: Oxford University Press.

Bogue, Carl W. 1975. *Jonathan Edwards and the covenant of grace.* Cherry Hill, NJ: Mack Publishing Company.

Bunyan, John. 1979. *Come and welcome to Jesus Christ*. In *The Miscellaneous Works of John Bunyan*, ed. Richard L. Greaves. Oxford: Clarendon Press.

Calvin, John. 1960. *The institutes of the Christian religion*, ed. John T. McNeill. Vols. 20 & 21. *The Library of Christian Classics*. Philadelphia: The Westminster Press.

Chauncy, Charles. 1784. *The benevolence of Deity: Fairly and impartially considered in three parts*. Ann Arbor: University Microfilms 1982; Boston: Power & Willis.

_____. [1743] 1975. *Seasonable thoughts on the state of religion in New England*. Reprint Edition. Hicksville, NY: Regina Press.

Cherry, Conrad. [1966] 1974. *Jonathan Edwards: A reappraisal*. Gloucester, MA: Peter Smith.

Clark, Gordon. [1952] 1960. *A Christian view of men and things*. The Payton Lectures, delivered in condensed form at Fuller Theological Seminary, 1951. Grand Rapids: Eerdmans.

Committee for Christian Education. n. d. See *The Westminster Standards* n. d.

Conforti, Joseph A. 1981. *Samuel Hopkins and the New Divinity movement*. Grand Rapids: Christian University Press.

Cotton, John. 1654. *The New Covenant*. London: Printed by Matthew Simons for Francis Egleffield & John Allen.

_____. 1671. *A Treatise on the Covenant of Grace*. 3d edition. London: For Peter Parker.

Cunningham, Charles E. 1942. *Timothy Dwight*. New York: The MacMillan Company.

Delattre, Roland Andre. 1968. *Beauty and sensibility in the thought of Jonathan Edwards: An essay in aesthetics and theological ethics*. New Haven: Yale University Press.

Dodds, Elisabeth D. [1971] 1976. *Marriage to a difficult man: The "uncommon union" of Jonathan and Sarah Edwards*. 2d printing. Philadelphia: Westminster Press.

Dwight, Timothy. 1863. *Theology explained and defended*. New York: Harper and Brothers, Publishers.

Edwards, Jonathan. 1879. *The works of Jonathan Edwards, A. M. with an essay on his genius and writings by Henry Rogers: and a memoir by Sereno E.*

Dwight. Revised and corrected by Edward Hickman. 2 vols. 12th edition. London: William Tegg & Co.

Erdt, Terrence. 1980. *Jonathan Edwards: Art and a sense of the heart*. Amhearst: University of Massachusetts Press.

Fiering, Norman. 1981. *Jonathan Edwards's moral thought in its British context*. Chapel Hill, NC: University of North Carolina Press.

_____. 1981. *Moral philosophy at seventeenth-century Harvard*. Chapel Hill, NC: University of North Carolina Press.

Finney, Charles G. 1878. *Lectures on systematic theology*, ed. J. H. Fairchild. Reprint. Grand Rapids: Wm. B. Eerdmans Publishing Company.

Foster, Frank H. [1907] 1987. *A genetic history of the New England theology*. New York: Garland Publishing, Inc.

Gerstner, John H. 1987. *Jonathan Edwards: A mini-theology*. Wheaton: Tyndale.

_____. 1976. An outline of the apologetics of Jonathan Edwards. Part II: The unity of god. *Bibliotheca Sacra* 133 (April-June): 99-107.

Hall, David D. 1968. *The antinomian controversy, 1636-1638*. Middletown, CT: Wesleyan University Press.

Haller, William. [1938] 1984. *The rise of Puritanism*. Philadelphia: University of Pennsylvania.

Hardman, Keith J. 1983. *The Spiritual Awakeners*. Chicago: Moody Press.

Haroutunian, Joseph. 1932. *Piety versus moralism: The passing of the New England theology*. New York: Holt.

Heimert, Alan. 1968. *Religion and the American mind*. Cambridge: Harvard University Press.

Heimert, Alan and Perry Miller, eds. 1967. *The Great Awakening: Documents illustrating the crisis and its consequences*. Indianapolis: Bobbs-Merrill.

Higgins, John R. 1984. Aspects of the doctrine of the Holy Spirit during the antinomian controversy of New England with special reference to John Cotton and Anne Hutchinson. Ph. D. diss. Westminster Theological Seminary, Philadelphia.

Hobbes, Thomas. 1958. *Leviathan parts I and II*. In *The Library of Liberal Arts*, 69, ed. Oskar Piest. Intro. Herbert W. Schneider. Indianapolis: The Bobbs-Merrill Company.

Holbrook, Clyde Amos. 1973. *The ethics of Jonathan Edwards: Morality and aesthetics*. Ann Arbor: University of Michigan Press.

Hutcheson, Francis. [1742] 1969. *An essay on the nature and conduct of the passions and affections with illustrations on the moral sense*. 3d edition. Facsimile. Intro. Paul McReynolds. Gainesville, FL: Scholars' Facsimiles & Reprints.

Knappen, M. M. [1939] 1966. *Tudor Puritanism: A chapter in the history of idealism*. 3d Impression. Chicago: University of Chicago Press.

Ladd, George Eldon. 1967. *The New Testament and criticism*. Grand Rapids: William B. Eerdmans Publishing Company.

Latourette, Kenneth Scott. 1953. *A History of Christianity*. New York: Harper and Row.

Lesser, M. X. 1981. *Jonathan Edwards: A reference guide*. Boston: G. K. Hall.

Letham, Robert. 1986. Early covenant theology. Class lectures. Westminster Theology Seminary, Philadelphia.

Lillback, Peter A. 1985. The binding of God: Calvin's role in the development of covenant theology. Ph. D. diss. Westminster Theological Seminary, Philadelphia.

Logan, Samuel T., Jr. 1984. The theology of Jonathan Edwards. Class lecture. 13 March. Westminster Theological Seminary, Philadelphia.

_____. 1986. Where have all the tulips gone? Inaugural address. Westminster Theological Seminary, Philadelphia.

Locke, John. 1952. *An Essay on human understanding*. Vol. 35, *Great Books of the Western World*, ed. Robert Maynard Hutchins, 85-395. Chicago: William Benton, 1952.

Lovelace, Richard. 1985. Edward's theology: Puritanism meets a new age. *Christian History* IV, No. 4:19.

Malebranche, Nicolas. 1700. *Father Malebranche's treatise concerning the search after truth. The whole work complete. To which is added the author's treatise of nature and grace: Being a consequence of the principles contained in the search*, trans. T. Taylor. 2d edition. London: W. Bowyer for Thomas Bennet, T. Leigh, and W. Midwinter.

Manspeaker, Nancy. 1981. *Jonathan Edwards: A bibliographical synopsis*. Lewiston, NY: E. Mellen Press.

Miller, Perry. [1949] 1973. *Jonathan Edwards*. Westport, CT: Greenwood Press.

_____. [1939] 1982. *The New England mind: The seventeenth century.* Cambridge: Harvard University Press.

_____. [1953] 1983. *The New England mind: From colony to province.* Reprint. Cambridge: Harvard University Press.

_____, ed. [1956] 1982. *The American Puritans: Their prose and their poetry.* New York: Columbia University Press.

Milton, John. [1949] 1961. *Paradise lost.* In *The Portable Milton*, ed. and intro. Douglas Bush. New York: Viking Press.

Morgan, Edmund S. 1958. *The Puritan dilemma: The story of John Winthrop.* Toronto: Little, Brown, and Company.

_____. [1963] 1982. *Visible Saints: The history of the Puritan idea.* 7th printing. Ithaca: Cornell University Press.

Murray, Iain. 1987. *Jonathan Edwards: A new biography.* Carlisle, PA: The Banner of Truth Trust.

O'Donovan, Oliver. 1980. *The problem of self-love in St. Augustine.* New Haven: Yale University Press.

Roberts, T. A. 1973. *The concept of benevolence: Aspects of eighteenth-century moral philosophy.* London: MacMillan.

Rolston, Holmes, III. 1972. *John Calvin versus the Westminster Confession.* Richmond, VA: John Knox Press.

Shaftesbury, Anthony Earl of. 1963. *Characteristics of men, manners, opinions, times, etc.* Edited, with an Introduction and Notes, by John M. Robertson. 2 Vols. Gloucester, MA: Peter Smith.

Simpson, Alan. [1955] 1966. *Puritanism in Old and New England.* Chicago: The University of Chicago Press.

Steele, David N. and Curtis C. Thomas. 1963. *The five points of Calvinism.* Phillipsburg, NJ: Presbyterian & Reformed Publishing Co.

The Westminster Standards. n. d. Published by Committee for Christian Education and Publications, 1020 Monticello Court, Montgomery, AL 36109.

Trinterud, Leonard J. 1949. *The forming of an American tradition.* Philadelphia: Westminster Press.

Tyner, Wayne Conrad. 1977. *The theology of Timothy Dwight in historical perspective.* Ann Arbor: University Microfilms.

Walker, Williston. [1918] 1959. *A history of the Christian church*. New York: Charles Scribner's Sons.

―――, ed. [1893] 1960. *The creeds and platforms of Congregationalism*. Philadelphia: Pilgrim Press.

Winslow, Ola. [1940] 1979. *Jonathan Edwards*. New York: Octagon Books.

Winthrop, John. 1908. *Winthrop's journal 1630-1649*, ed. J. Franklin Jameson. New York: Charles Scribner's Sons.

Wright, Conrad. 1955. *The beginnings of Unitarianism in America*. Boston: Starr King Press.

Zwingli, Ulrich. [1929] 1981. *Commentary on true and false religion*, ed. Samuel Macauley Jackson and Clarence Nevin Heller. Durham, NC: Labyrinth Press.

INDEX

aesthetics
  church membership and, 21
  Edwards's conversion and, 15
  ethics and, 27-28, 46-47, 60-65
  primary beauty, 21, 46, 63
  Sarah Pierrepont and, 19-20
Ames, William
  covenantal theology of, 92-93, 98-99
  influence on John Robinson, 6
  on metaphysics, 24-25
  on self-love, 37
  on voluntarism, 33-34
  work: *Marrow of Theology*, 92, 99
antinomianism, 8, 89-91, 104, 105, 108, 113
Aristotle, 32-33, 34, 41, 47
Arminianism, 22, 89-90, 105. *See also* Dort: canons of
  definition of, 4
  development of, 112-18
  in Dwight's theology, 137-43
  tendency of, 102, 104, 105, 108, 156
  threat of, 79-80, 111
Augustine, 37, 41, 53
  eudaemonism, 35-36
  on divine self-love, 36
  on moral inability, 82
  voluntarism of, 34-35

"Author of sin" idea, 120-21, 138. See also *Sin ... an Advantage to the Universe*
beatific, 1, 23
  as ongoing reality, 16
  basis for beauty, 60
  Calvinistic framework of, 15, 86
  corporate image of, 21
  definition of, 3
  ethics based on, 59
  humbling effect of, 16, 73
  key to ignition of Great Awakening, 20-21
  observed in Sarah Pierrepont, 19-20
  relationship to theology, 108-9
  scriptural nature of, 15
Beecher, Lyman, 130, 143
"being in general." *See* Ontology
Bellamy, Joseph, 4, 124
  governmental atonement, 128
  work: *Wisdom of God in the Permission of Sin*, 127
benevolence
  Augustine on, 36
  Chauncy on, 117-23
  definition of, 3
  Dwight on, 131-37
  Edwards on, 61-63, 136-37
  Edwards's resolution of, 17
  Hobbes on, 41-42
  Hume on, 52

benevolence (*continued*)
    Hutcheson on, 48-49
    public benevolence, 44-45
    reflected in Sarah Pierrepont, 19
    Shaftesbury on, 46
Bentley, William, 124
Berkeley, Bishop George, 38, 56
Bradford, William, 6
Brainerd, David, 20
Brattle, William, 54
Brattle Street Church, 111
Buell, Samuel, 4, 20, 124
Bunyan, John, 66, 83
    work: *Come and Welcome to Jesus Christ*, 66, 83
Butler, Joseph, 52
Calvin, John, 6. *See also* Calvinism
    on faith, 106
    on "fitness," 108
    on self-love, 36-37
    on "sense of the heart," 89
    on the law, 97-98, 100
    on Word and Spirit, 14-15
Calvinism. *See also* Calvin, John; Dort: canons of
    covenantal theology consistent with, 89-91, 97-98, 100
    definition of, 4
    Edwards's conversion characterized by, 12-15
    Edwards's rationale for, 81, 103-104
    Edwards's theology characterized by, 79-84
    objectivism provided by, 79
Cambridge Platform, 8
Cartesian, 3-4, 37, 41, 119
Chauncy, Charles, 31
    leader of Old Lights, 112-23
    works: *Benevolence of the Deity*, 117-23
        Seasonable Thoughts, 113, 114
        Salvation for All Men, 115-16, 129
Christ as Second Adam, 101-104
College of New Jersey. See New Jersey, College of

Colman, Benjamin, 80, 112-13
complacence, 48, 61-62, 76, 134-35
Congregationalists, 6, 8, 127
"Consistent Calvinists," 4, 124-30
consociation movement, 8-9
conversion. *See also* Regeneration; Faith; Narrative of grace
    Puritan "root of the matter," 5-6
    at Northampton revival, 80
    of Augustine, 34
    of Edwards, 10-15
    relationship to narrative of grace, 9
Cooper, Anthony Ashley. *See* Shaftesbury, Third Earl of
Cotton, John, 90
    introduced narrative of grace, 7
    on covenant of works, 101
    on faith and covenant condition, 104-106
    on revelation, 13-14
covenant. *See also* Miller, Perry: errors; Imputation of Adam's sin; Law; Trinity
    Abrahamic, 96, 97
    church, 6, 21
    Davidic, 96, 97
    Half-Way, 8, 21, 130
    national, 7-8
    Noahic, 96
    of grace, 90-91, 94-97, 99, 102, 104
    of redemption, 92-96
    of works, 8, 51, 90-91, 98-102, 104, 142
    with Israel, 96-97
Cromwell, Oliver, 5-6
Cutler, Timothy, 11, 17
Darrow, Clarence, 23
Davenport, James, 112
    enthusiasm, 31, 50, 113
    Confessions and Retractions, 113
Decrees, 82-83, 92-94, 149-52. *See also* Sovereignty, divine
    Dwight's weakening of, 139-40
Descartes, Rene, 3-4, 11, 37-38, 42. *See also* Cartesian

disinterested benevolence
    Dwight vs. Edwards on, 133-37
    Edwards on, 65-71
    Hopkins on, 125-26
    Hutcheson on, 47-48
    Shaftesbury on, 46, 47, 48, 137
Dort. *See also* Calvinism;
        Arminianism
    Canons of, 4, 81-84
        Dwight's compromising of, 137-43
        Edwards's espousal of, 81-84
    Synod of, 4
Dwight, Sereno, 17-18
Dwight, Timothy
    Arminianism, 137-43
    benevolism, 131-37
    catalyst for Second Great Awakening, 130-31
    lectures: *Theology Explained and Defended*, 131
    utilitarianism, 133, 135, 137
Edwards, Jonathan
    birth, 9
    conversion, 10, 11-15, 17
    death, 21
    dismissed from Northampton, 9, 20-21
    marriage, 18
    pastor at New York, 11, 15, 17
    pastor at Northampton, 9, 18-21
    philosopher, 2, 19-20, 25-29, 50, 53-54
    president, College of New Jersey, 21
    revival at Northampton, 20-22, 52, 80
    Stockbridge period of ministry, 21, 22
    student at Yale, 11
    tutor at Yale, 17-18
    works: *Charity and Its Fruits*, 72
        Freedom of the Will, 22, 51, 57
        God Glorified in Man's Dependence, 81, 103-104
        God's End in Creation, 22-23, 38, 58-59

History of the Work of Redemption, 22, 25, 26-27, 95
Justification by Faith, 93
Narrative of the Surprising Work of God, 21, 52, 80, 131
Nature of True Virtue, 22-23, 31, 38-39, 48-49, 53, 59-64
"Notes on the Mind," 17-18, 28
Original Sin, 22, 40, 51, 53
Qualifications for Communion, 21, 96
Religious Affections, 17, 21-22, 31-32, 47, 50-51, 113
"Sinners in the Hands of an Angry God," 23
Edwards, Jonathan, Jr., 4, 124, 129
    Dwight's mentor, 139
Edwards, Sarah. *See* Pierrepont, Sarah
end. *See also* Motive
    God's
        in Chauncy's system, 121
        in Dwight's system, 133
        in Edwards's system, 58-59
        in Hopkins's system, 128
        in Malebranche's system, 38
"enthusiasm," 31, 38, 43, 50, 113
eudaemonism, 35, 71. *See also* Happiness
faith
    as act, 105, 106-108
    as consent to being, 61-63
    as condition, 83, 104-106
    as duty, 142
    as habit, 105, 106
    as instrument, 106, 107
    as uniting with Christ, 107-08
federal theology. *See* Covenant: theology
Fall of man, 95, 99. *See also* Covenant: of works; Imputation of Adam's sin
    Dwight's view of, 139
    Edwards's view of, 40, 51, 99, 101-102
    in lapsarian issue, 149-52
    Malebranche's view of, 40

"Farmer Metaphysicians." *See* Consistent Calvinists; Bentley, William
Finney, Charles G., 130, 131
"fitness," 107, 108
Garden, Alexander, 111
general atonement, 140
governmental atonement. *See* Grotius
Great Awakening, 20, 21, 22, 79, 111-15, 130
Grotius
   governmental atonement, 128-29
Half-Way Covenant. *See* Covenant: Half-Way
happiness
   Augustine on, 35-36
   Chauncy on, 121-22
   Dwight on, 133
   Edwards on, 69-71, 76-77
Harvard College
   Edwards's father matriculated at, 9
   Marrow of Theology standard reading at, 92
   new moral philosophy taught at, 54
   opposition to Awakening centered at, 115
   technologia expounded at, 24-25
   Whitefield preached at, 111-12
heaven, 13, 17
hedonism, 69-70
   psychological, 69
Heereboord, Adrian, 108. *See also* Fitness
hell, 23-24, 46-47, 129
Hobbes, Thomas, 44, 45-46, 47
   Leviathan, 41
   on human self-interest motive, 41-42
holiness, 46-47, 64-65, 66, 73-77
   God's moral attribute, 75
   lacking in Dwight's theology, 131-32, 142
Hopkins, Samuel, 4, 20, 44, 61, 124-28
   heir of Edwards's manuscripts, 125

   works: *A Dialogue between a Calvinist and a Semi-Calvinist*, 125
   Inquiry into the Promises of the Gospel, 127
   On the Necessity of the Knowledge of God's Law in order to the Knowledge of Sin, 128
   Sin ... an Advantage to the Universe, 126
   The Nature of True Holiness, 125-26
Hopkinsians. *See* Consistent Calvinists
Hume, David, 46, 47, 52-53
Hutcheson, Francis, 37, 40-41, 46, 53, 54, 60
   opposed to Locke, 47
   utilitarianism, 47
   views on ethics and theology, 47-52
Hutchinson, Ann, 8, 90-91, 105
imputation of Adam's Sin, 51, 98-99, 115, 122
   Dwight's rejection of, 138
infralapsarianism, 149-52
intellectualism, 3, 52, 113-14
irresistible grace, 4, 83
   Dwight's dissatisfaction with, 140-42
   Dwight's inversion of, 138
justification, 56, 80, 84, 102-103, 105-108
Knox, John, 6
law, 97-101
limited atonement, 4, 83
Locke, John, 11, 17-18, 38, 47
   influence on Edwards, 43-45
   on human self-interest motive, 44-46
   sensationism, 42
   rejection of innate ideas, 42-43
   work: *Essay on Human Understanding*, 17-18, 42
Malebranche, Nicolas, 37-41, 55-56
   on divine self-love, 39
   on God's principal end, 38
   on the Fall, 40

Malebranche, Nicolas (*continued*)
    work: *Search After Truth*, 38
Marrow of Theology. *See* Ames, William
Mather, Cotton, 8
Mayhew, Jonathan, 115, 122
    Arminianism embraced by, 115, 115-17
    benevolism of, 116-17
    friend of John Adams, 122
    works: *Seven Sermons*, 117
        Nature, Extent, and Perfection of the Divine Goodness, 117
        Striving to enter in at the Strait gate ..., 127
means of grace, 86, 125-27, 142-43
metaphysics, 43, 119, 126
    Edwards's regard for, 25-29, 83-88
    "Farmer Metaphysicians," 124
    in Puritanism, 24-25
Miller, Perry, 2, 17-18, 22, 56-57
    errors:
        concerning Arminianism in New England, 80
        concerning Edwards's covenant theology, 92-104
        concerning Edwards's discovery of Locke, 17-18
        concerning Locke's influence on Edwards, 43-45
        concerning origin of covenant theology, 89-91
Mills, Jedediah
    Inquiry into the State of the Unregenerate under the Gospel, 127
monism, 84-85, 87-89
moral fitness. *See* Fitness
moral inability, 51, 82, 138-39, 141-42
moral necessity, 56, 83
Morton, Charles, 54, 108
motive, 41, 44, 57 *See also* End
    of God, 58-59
    of man, 65-68
mysticism, 13, 33, 86-87, 126
"narrative of grace," 7, 9, 21

natural ability, 51, 141
Neoplatonism. *See* Platonism
"New Divinity," 4, 127. *See also* Consistent Calvinists; Hopkins, Samuel
New Jersey, College of, 21, 125
New Lights, 112, 124-25
New Side, 112-13
Niles, Samuel. *See also* Imputation of Adam's sin
    work: *True Doctrine of Original Sin*, 122
Old Lights, 112, 124-25
Old Side, 112-13
ontology
    being in general, 61-63, 84-87, 126
    being simply considered, 62, 134-35
    benevolent being, 62
    of Augustine, 36
    of Edwards, 61-64
    of Malebranche, 39
Paine, Thomas, 130
panentheism, 84-88
pantheism, 84-85
Perkins, William, 6, 92
perseverence of the saints, 4, 56, 84, 142
Pierrepont, James, 18
Pierrepont, Sara, 18-20
Platonism
    compatible with affectional religion, 33
    Neoplatonism, 34, 84-89
Presbyterians of Middle Colonies
    Old Side/NewSide controversy, 112
    relationship to Saybrook Platform, 8-9
Preston, John, 92
primary beauty. *See* Aesthetics
Princeton College. *See* New Jersey, College of
Ramus, Peter, 24-25
regeneration, 12-13, 21, 27, 36, 43, 47. *See also* Conversion; Narrative of grace

Richardson, Alexander, 24-25, 33, 34
Robinson, John, 6
Savoy Declaration, 127
Saybrook
    Platform, 8-9
    Confession, 17
Second Great Awakening, 130-31
self-love
    divine, 2, 36, 39, 55, 59-60, 135, 136
    God's self-love as a model for man, 72-75
    human, 2, 35-37, 39-40, 44-45, 48, 67-75
        forms of, 71-72
"sense of the heart," 10, 12, 43, 89
    Hutcheson's "Internal Sense," 47-49
Shaftesbury, Third Earl of, 37, 38, 40-41, 46-48
    benevolist propositions, 46
    union of ethics and aesthetics, 46-47
    "disinterest" vs. "uninterest," 137
Shepherd, Thomas, 108. *See also* Fitness
Sin . . . an advantage to the Universe, 126, 138. *See also* Hopkins, Samuel
sovereignty, divine, 4, 51, 57, 59, 86-87, 119, 139
    and moral inability, 51
    basis for Edwards's ethics, 59
    in Edwards's conversion, 11-13, 56
Stiles, Ezra
    Yale president, 131
Stoddard, Solomon, 8-9, 18, 20-21
Stoicism, 140
Stowe, Harriet Beecher
    on Consistent Calvinism, 130
Summa, 88-89, 95, 147
supralapsarianism, 149-52
Taylor, John, 22, 81, 115. *See also* Armnianism
    Scripture-Doctrine of Original Sin, 115

Taylor, Nathaniel, 130, 143
"technologia," 24-25
Tennent, Gilbert, 112-13
    sermon: "The Danger of an Unconverted Ministry," 113
Tertullian, 24
total depravity, 4, 51, 82, 119-20
    Chauncy's denial of, 119-20
    Dwight's compromise on, 140-41
    Mayhew's rejection of, 117
Trinity
    Ames on, 92-93
    Augustine's view of, 36
    Dwight on, 134-35
    Edwards's delight in, 20
    Edwards's view of, 59-60, 63, 93-96
Two Dissertations, 61, 88-89
unconditional election, 4, 11-13, 82-83, 139-40, 151. *See also* Decrees
unitarianism, 3, 111, 112, 115-17, 130
utilitarianism
    adopted by Chauncy, 118, 121-22
    in Dwight's theology, 133, 135, 137
    principles laid by Hutcheson, 47
visible saints concept, 7-8
voluntarism, 34-35, 37, 113-14
Webster, Samuel. *See also* Imputation of Adam's sin
    work: *Winter Evening's Conversation Upon the Doctrine of Original Sin*, 122, 127
Wesley, John, 9, 79
Westminster
    Catechisms, 11, 23, 65, 76
    Confession, 98-101
    Standards, 8
Whitefield, George, 20, 79, 111
Williams, Israel, 80
"willingness to be damned" doctrine, 52, 72, 137
    Hopkin's espousal of, 125
Winthrop, John, 5, 6, 108-109
Wise, John, 122

Yale College
    Edwards a tutor at, 17-18
    Edwards enters, 11
    Edwardseans among graduates of, 115
    James Pierrepont's role in founding, 18
    Marrow standard reading at, 92
    revival at, 130-31
    Whitefield observes spiritual deadness at, 112

Zwingli, Ulrich, 36, 37